Managing Editor
Karen Goldfluss, M.S. Ed.

Editor-in-Chief
Sharon Coan, M.S. Ed.

Illustrator
Renée Christine Yates

Cover Artist
Barb Lorseyedi

Art Manager
Kevin Barnes

Art Director
CJae Froshay

Imaging
Rosa C. See

Product Manager
Phil Garcia

Publisher
Mary D. Smith, M.S. Ed.

Author

Lorin Klistoff, M.A.

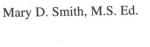

Teacher Created Resources, Inc.
6421 Industry Way
Westminster, CA 92683
www.teachercreated.com.

ISBN-0-7439-3172-6

©2004 Teacher Created Resources, Inc.

Reprinted, 2006

Made in U.S.A.

Table of Contents

Introduction

Culture

- Pilgrims
- Christopher Columbus
- George Washington
- Abraham Lincoln
- Martin Luther King, Jr.

- Susan B. Anthony
- Harriet Tubman
- Rosa Parks
- Pocahontas
- Christopher Columbus
- Martin Luther King, Jr.
- George Washington
- Abraham Lincoln
- Johnny Appleseed

- Classroom
- School
- Neighborhood
- Community

- North America
- World
- United States

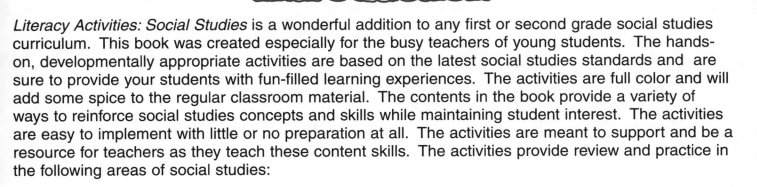

Introduction

Literacy Activities: Social Studies is a wonderful addition to any first or second grade social studies curriculum. This book was created especially for the busy teachers of young students. The hands-on, developmentally appropriate activities are based on the latest social studies standards and are sure to provide your students with fun-filled learning experiences. The activities are full color and will add some spice to the regular classroom material. The contents in the book provide a variety of ways to reinforce social studies concepts and skills while maintaining student interest. The activities are easy to implement with little or no preparation at all. The activities are meant to support and be a resource for teachers as they teach these content skills. The activities provide review and practice in the following areas of social studies:

- reasons that Americans celebrate certain national holidays

- important buildings, statues, monuments, and symbols that are tied with state and national history

- picture timelines

- beginning, middle, and end of historical stories

- key figures and roles they played in national history

- comparisons of items from now and long ago

- the importance and the reasons for rules and that when rules are not followed, consequences will follow

- the political system of the U.S. and opportunity for participation

- the many types of transportation used to move people and products

- the origin of food items found in the local stores by tracing their routes from place of origin

- the effects of specialization and interdependence of people

- the use of a map key to interpret symbols and cardinal directions to locate places

- names and locations of continents, countries in North America, oceans, and the United States

Each activity is set up with an easy-to-follow lesson. First, each lesson states the objective or learning skill and the materials needed. Most of the materials are provided inside this book. Next, the lesson outlines what kinds of groupings can be implemented with each activity. Most of the activities can be adapted in multiple ways and can be "custom tailored." They can be implemented as a whole-class lesson, in small group, for partners, independently, or in a center. The activities can also be adapted for a variety of student levels. Suggestions are listed in the actual directions of the activity or they are suggested in the "Ideas" section. The "Ideas" section contains many helpful hints on such things as storage of materials or ideas to either enhance or extend the activity. Overall, the book is an asset to any first- or second-grade teacher.

Holiday Riddler

Skill

* understands the reasons that Americans celebrate certain national holidays

Student Grouping

* partners
* small group
* large group

Materials

* copy of Holiday Riddler student answer sheet (page 5) for each student
* Holiday Riddler Cards (pages 7 and 9)
* Holiday Choices chart (page 11)
* Holiday Riddler Answers (page 13)
* writing utensil for each student

Directions

1. Hand each student a Holiday Riddler student answer sheet.
2. Tell them that you (or another student) will be reading a Holiday Riddler question and they must guess the correct answer. In addition, tell them that they must write the answer next to the appropriate number on their papers. For instance, if a riddle is labeled as Riddle 7, then they must place the answer to the question next to the number 7 on their papers.
3. Tell students that they can use the Holiday Choices chart to help them guess a correct answer. (*Note:* If you are implementing this activity with a large group, write the choices from the Holiday Choices chart on a chalkboard or whiteboard or copy a chart for each student. For early readers, go over each holiday name on the chart. Then proceed with the activity.)
4. Place all Holiday Riddler Cards in a pile facedown.
5. Have a student pick a card. Then read the riddle (or if you have a fluent reader, have him or her read the riddle).
6. Have each student write his or her answer to the riddle on the correct blank on the student answer sheet.
7. After all the Holiday Riddler Cards are finished, read the answers from the Holiday Riddler Answers card.
8. Have students discuss their answers together.

Ideas

* Laminate the Holiday Riddler Cards, Holiday Choices chart, and the Holiday Riddler Answers card.
* Give students calendars to help them guess the holiday riddles.
* Have a student pick a holiday that is of interest to him or her and write an in-depth report. Have each student give a brief oral presentation of his or her report in front of the class. Encourage each student to pick a holiday that his or her family celebrates.
* Keep a classroom calendar that marks all the holidays your students celebrate.

Holiday Riddler

January 1

February 14

President's Day

March 17

Easter

Memorial Day

Flag Day

July 4

December 25

Thanksgiving Day

Veteran's Day

October 31

Colombus Day

Labor Day

1._____

2._____

3._____

4._____

5._____

6._____

7._____

8._____

9._____

10._____

11._____

12._____

13._____

14._____

15._____

16._____

5

Holiday Riddler Cards

Riddle 1
This day arrives on February 14 every year. It is a time to celebrate love, caring, and sharing. What day am I?

Riddle 2
This holiday is celebrated as a new beginning, a time to start over. In the U.S. it is celebrated on January 1. What day am I?

Riddle 3
This day was first celebrated in Plymoth colony. The harvest was so good that the Pilgrims were thankful and invited their Native American friends to eat. What day am I?

Riddle 4
This day celebrates the explorer who discovered the New World in 1492. What day am I?

Riddle 5
Long ago the Celts celebrated this day on October 31. At night, they carried lanterns and wore disguises to keep from being recognized by the spirits. What day am I?

Riddle 6
This day is celebrated on the first Monday in September to honor American workers. What day am I?

Riddle 7
This day is the United States' birthday. In 1776 an important paper called the Declaration of Independence was signed. This day is also known as Independence Day. What

Riddle 8
This is the day Americans honor those who have died for their country. It is celebrated on the last Monday in May. What day am I?

©Teacher Created Resources, Inc.   #3172 Social Studies Literacy Activities

#3172 Social Studies Literacy Activities

©*Teacher Created Resources, Inc.*

Holiday Riddler Cards

Riddle 9
On this day the idea is to play a trick on someone. It is the first day in April. What day am I?

Riddle 10
For Christians, this day celebrates Jesus rising from the dead. People celebrate with eating, a visit to a bunny, or decorate eggs. What day am I?

Riddle 11
This day is named after a saint in Ireland and is celebrated in March. Shamrocks and the color green are usually seen on this holiday. What day am I?

Riddle 12
This day is celebrated on the third Monday in February. It is a day to remember presidents of the United States. What day am I?

Riddle 13
This day is celebrated on the third Monday in January to honor the life of Martin Luther King, Jr. What day am I?

Riddle 14
This day celebrates the birth of Jesus. Santa and giving gifts are also known for this holiday. What day am I?

Riddle 15
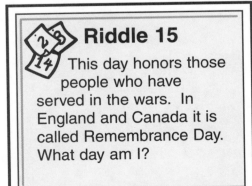
This day honors those people who have served in the wars. In England and Canada it is called Remembrance Day. What day am I?

Riddle 16
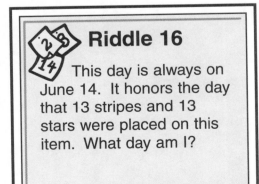
This day is always on June 14. It honors the day that 13 stripes and 13 stars were placed on this item. What day am I?

#3172 Social Studies Literacy Activities

Holiday Choices

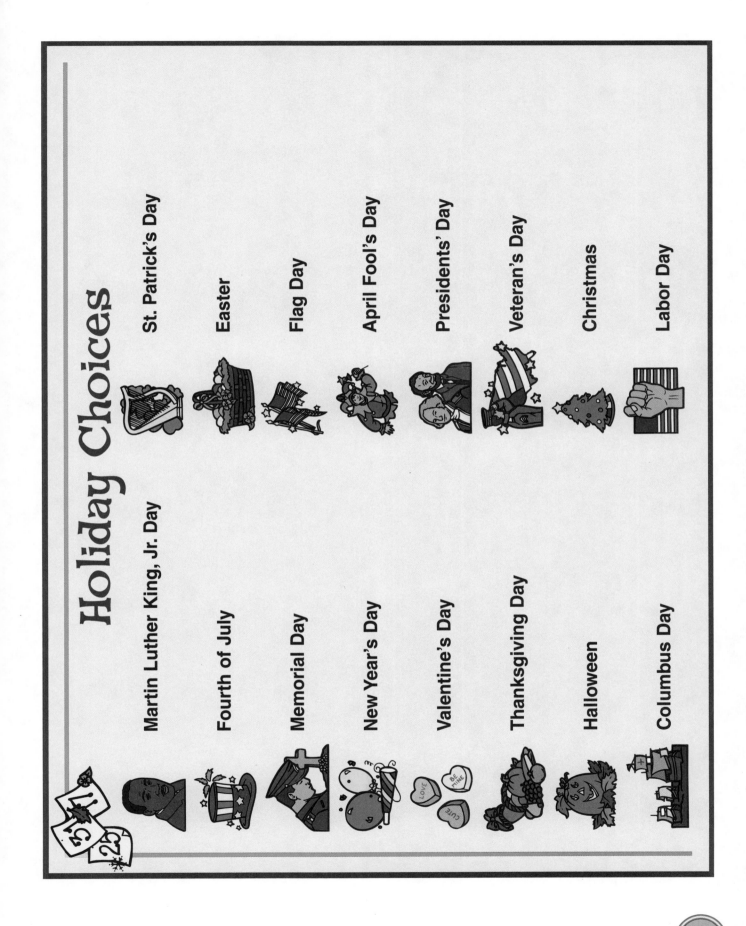

Martin Luther King, Jr. Day

Fourth of July

Memorial Day

New Year's Day

Valentine's Day

Thanksgiving Day

Halloween

Columbus Day

St. Patrick's Day

Easter

Flag Day

April Fool's Day

Presidents' Day

Veteran's Day

Christmas

Labor Day

#3172 Social Studies Literacy Activities

Holiday Riddler Answers

1. Valentine's Day

2. New Year's Day

3. Thanksgiving Day

4. Columbus Day

5. Halloween

6. Labor Day

7. Fourth of July

8. Memorial Day

9. April Fool's Day

10. Easter

11. St. Patrick's Day

12. Presidents' Day

13. Martin Luther King, Jr. Day

14. Christmas

15. Veteran's Day

16. Flag Day

#3172 Social Studies Literacy Activities

#3172 Social Studies Literacy Activities

Monumental Bingo

Skill

* knows why important buildings, statues, and monuments are tied with state and national history
* knows the history of American symbols

Student Grouping

* partners
* small group
* large group

Materials

* Bingo Cards (pages 17 and 19)
* Bingo Mats (pages 21, 23, and 25) for each student
* markers—such as plastic circular chips or pennies

Directions

1. Give a Bingo Mat to each student (or set of partners).
2. Give each student (or set of partners) a small pile of markers.
3. Mix up the Bingo Cards and place face down.
4. Tell students that if the name on the card you read matches a place or item on their Bingo Mat, they may place a marker on it. Tell them that if they get three markers in a row going vertically, horizontally, or diagonally, they must call out "Bingo." Remind all students that they may place a marker on the middle square that reads "Free Space."
5. Pick one card from the pile and read the description. Before actually giving the name of the monument, building, or symbol, have students try to guess the answer. Tell them to look at their mats for any clues. After a short time of guessing, read the name.
6. If students have the name on their Bingo Mat, they may place a marker on top of the square.
7. Continue reading one card at a time until somebody says, "Bingo."

Ideas

* Laminate Bingo Cards and Bingo Mats.
* "Blackout" can be played where the player must have his or her entire card covered with markers.
* Emphasize key words in the Bingo Cards to help students find the answers.

Bingo Cards

This place is named in honor of Abraham Lincoln, one of our great presidents. A huge statue of Abraham Lincoln sitting in a chair is inside this memorial.

Lincoln Memorial

This place was built to help remember George Washington, the "Father of our Country." It is a very tall building.

Washington Monument

Americans make this promise to be loyal to our country.

Pledge of Allegiance

This statue was presented to the United States by France. It sits in New York Harbor. It shows a woman with chains at her feet and her right hand holding a burning torch that represents liberty or freedom.

Statue of Liberty

This is our nation's song and was written by Francis Scott Key.

Star-Spangled Banner

This animal is seen as a symbol of freedom, strength, and courage. It is America's national symbol.

Bald Eagle

This area is the capital of the United States. It is not a state. D.C. stands for District of Columbia.

Washington, D.C.

This is the building where the current president lives. It has three floors. All the presidents have lived here except George Washington. The president's office is called the Oval Office.

White House

#3172 Social Studies Literacy Activities

Bingo Cards

This item is a symbol of the United States. It has 50 stars and 13 stripes. The 50 stars stand for the 50 states. The 13 stripes stand for the 13 original colonies.

The U.S. Flag

This building was built to honor Thomas Jefferson. It is circular, with 26 columns around it. The ceiling is dome-shaped.

Jefferson Memorial

This item symbolizes American freedom from Britain. It was rung on July 8, 1776, in Philadelphia after an important paper, the Declaration of Independence, was read.

The Liberty Bell

The United States Congress meets here. It has a dome. A sculpture of a woman sits on the top of the dome.

Capitol Building

This memorial was built to honor those soldiers in the United States Marine Corps who died in battle. It shows soldiers raising an American flag.

Marine Corps Memorial

This memorial is in the Black Hills of South Dakota. It has the heads of George Washington, Thomas Jefferson, Abraham Lincoln, and Theodore Roosevelt carved out of rock.

Mount Rushmore

This place was created to spread peace between countries. It has a colorful display of flags belonging to the different countries that are members.

The United Nations

No one knows how this character was created. It is said that this character was named after Samuel Wilson. The character stands for the government.

Uncle Sam

©*Teacher Created Resources, Inc.*

#3172 Social Studies Literacy Activities

Bingo Mats

Bingo Mats

#3172 Social Studies Literacy Activities

#3172 Social Studies Literacy Activities

©*Teacher Created Resources, Inc.*

Bingo Mats

A Timeline of Events

Skill

* knows how to develop picture time lines
* knows how to identify the beginning, middle, and end of historical stories

Student Grouping

* independent
* partners
* small group
* large group

Materials

* Copy the three-event timeline (page 29) or five-event timeline (page 31) for each student.
* Copy the appropriate set of event cards (Pilgrims–page 33, Christopher Columbus–page 35, George Washington–page 37, Abraham Lincoln–page 39, or Martin Luther King, Jr.–page 41) for each student. (*Note:* If students are using the three-event timeline, tell them to cut off and discard the bottom portion of their event card page. Tell them they will only be working with the top three cards.)

Directions

1. Give students the appropriate blank timeline (three-event timeline or five-event timeline). Tell them to make note of the words in the box, such as *beginning* or *first*.

2. Give students the appropriate set of event cards (Pilgrims, Christopher Columbus, George Washington, Abraham Lincoln, or Martin Luther King, Jr.).

3. Tell students that they are to place the event cards in the correct place on the timeline starting with the first event that occurred.

4. Read the cards together or have a fluent reader read them.

5. Have students try to place them in the correct order on the timeline.

6. Check the students' placement of event cards to make sure he or she understands the chronological order of events.

7. Have students read together the cards in chronological order.

Ideas

* Laminate timelines and cards and keep in a center for independent practice.
* Be sure to model how to put the cards and timeline together. Tell students to think through what would come first, second, etc. Start with the three-event timeline first. Then progress to the five-event timeline.
* Have students create picture timelines of their own lives or their families' histories using the timeline as a model.

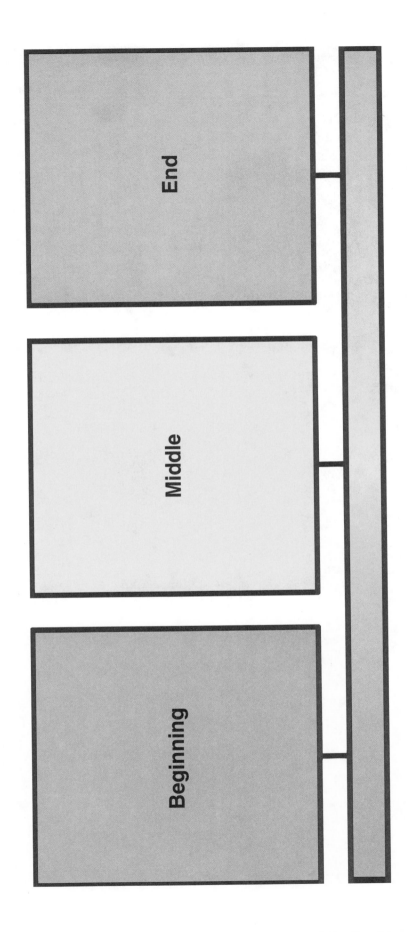

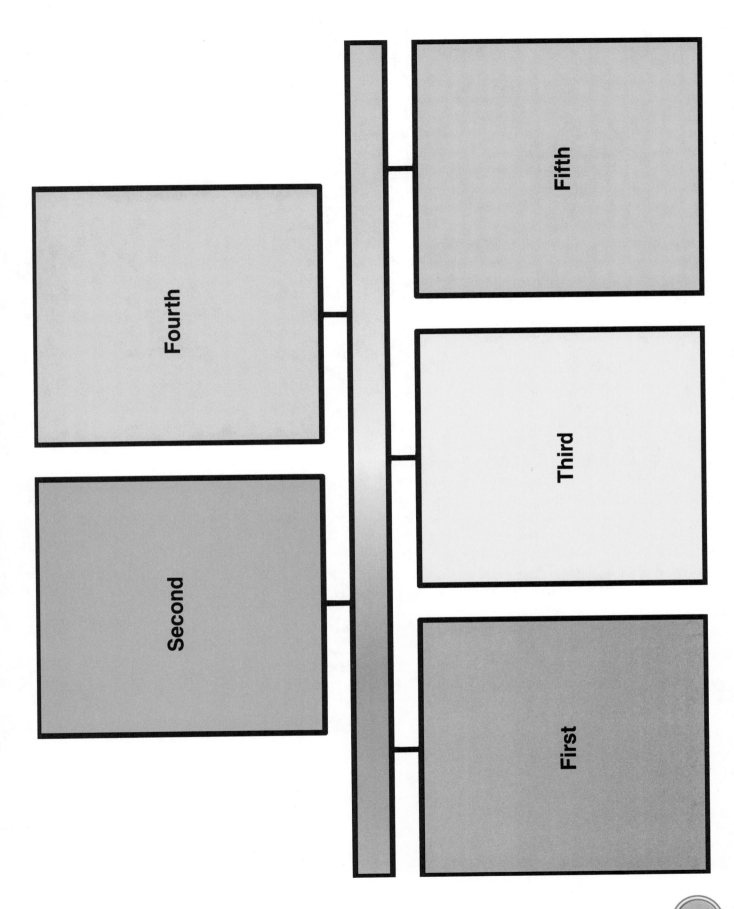

#3172 Social Studies Literacy Activities

©*Teacher Created Resources, Inc.*

Pilgrims

Cards for Three-Event Timeline

In 1863, Thanksgiving became a national holiday to remember the Pilgrims.

In 1621, the fall harvest was very good. The Pilgrims were so thankful that they invited their Native American friends to a feast.

In the year 1620, the Pilgrims sailed from England to look for the New World on the ship called the *Mayflower*.

Extra Cards for Five-Event Timeline

The Pilgrims became friends with the Native Americans. They helped the Pilgrims learn how to hunt better and how to plant crops.

The Pilgrims landed near Plymoth Rock and started to build homes. The first winter many people died because there wasn't enough food to eat.

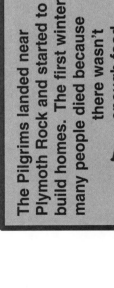

#3172 Social Studies Literacy Activities

Christopher Columbus

Cards for Three-Event Timeline

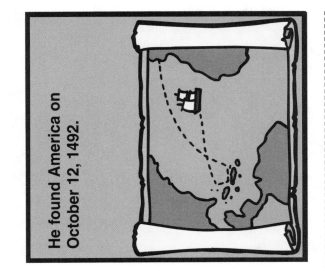

He found America on October 12, 1492.

In August, 1492, Columbus sailed with three ships to find gold and spices in the Indies.

Christopher Columbus was born in Genoa, Italy, in 1451.

Extra Cards for Five-Event Timeline

In the United States, we celebrate the second Monday of October as Columbus Day to remember his great voyage.

Columbus asked King Ferdinand and Queen Isabella to pay for his trip to reach India. They agreed.

George Washington

Cards for Three-Event Timeline

America became the United States of America. George Washington was elected the first president of the United States in 1789.

George Washington was the general of the American army during the Revolutionary War. He wanted America to be a separate country, not part of England.

George Washington was born on February 22, 1732 in Virginia. America was still a colony of England then.

VIRGINIA

Extra Cards for Five-Event Timeline

George Washington was called the "Father of Our Country." The Washington Monument was built to help us remember him.

George Washington married Martha Custis. She had two children.

Abraham Lincoln

Cards for Three-Event Timeline

Abraham Lincoln was shot and killed after the war ended in 1865. The people of the United States were sad.

Abraham Lincoln was elected president of the United States in 1860. The Civil War started, and he wanted the slaves to be free. He wanted to help keep the United States together.

Abraham Lincoln was born on February 12, 1809. He was born in a log cabin in Kentucky.

Extra Cards for Five-Event Timeline

Abraham Lincoln will always be remembered. The Lincoln Memorial honors him.

Abraham Lincoln became a lawyer. He married Mary Todd in 1842. They had four children.

Martin Luther King, Jr.

Sadly, Dr. King was killed in 1968. To honor his memory and work, we celebrate Martin Luther King, Jr. Day.

Dr. King began to work to change laws that were not fair. He made his famous speech in Washington, D.C., in 1963. It began with, "I have a dream."

Martin Luther King, Jr. was born in Atlanta, Georgia, on January 15, 1929. His father was a minister and his mother was a teacher.

Extra Cards for Five-Event Timeline

In December 1964, Dr. King was awarded the Nobel Peace Prize for his work.

While going to college, Martin met a woman named Coretta Scott. They got married on June 18, 1953.

#3172 Social Studies Literacy Activities

Face to Facts

Skill

* understands how important figures were significant to the history of democracy (Susan B. Anthony, Harriet Tubman, Rosa Parks, Pocahontas, Christopher Columbus, Martin Luther King, Jr., George Washington, Abraham Lincoln, and Johnny Appleseed)

Student Grouping

* individual
* partners
* small group
* large group
* center

Materials

* Face Cards (pages 45–61)
* Fact Cards (pages 63–67)
* Face to Facts Answer Key (page 69)
* tape (*optional*)

Directions

1. Post the Face Cards in a place where all students can see them. (Optional: You may want to tape the Face Cards on the wall for all to see.)

2. Tell students to look over each of the faces. Read the name of each person. Let students reveal to you what they already know about any of the faces.

3. Tell them that you are going to read a fact, and they must find the face that matches the fact. Tell them that two fact cards go with every face.

4. Mix up the Fact Cards and place in a pile facedown.

5. Pick a Fact Card and read to the students.

6. Have students try to make a guess about whose face the fact should go under.

7. Place the fact in the correct place under the face card. Use the Answer Key for a reference if you or another student should need a reference for the correct answers.

8. Play until all cards are finished.

Ideas

* Laminate Answer Key, Face Cards, and Fact Cards for durability.

* Have students add more fact cards to the wall or board.

* Have students chose another important historical person and find facts on him or her. Have each student make a portrait of the person, too. Add the portrait and facts to the wall with the other Face and Fact Cards.

* Create an interactive bulletin board. Hang the Face Cards in a place that can be easily accessible to students. Place an envelope with the Fact Cards in it. Have students choose a card throughout the day and place it under the correct person.

* Use the Face Cards to support other social studies lessons.

Susan B. Anthony

1820–1906

Born in Adams, Massachusetts

#3172 Social Studies Literacy Activities

Harriet Tubman

Circa 1820–1913
Born in Bucktown, Maryland

#3172 Social Studies Literacy Activities

©*Teacher Created Resources, Inc.*

Rosa Parks

Born 1913-2005
Born in Tuskegee, Alabama

#3172 Social Studies Literacy Activities

©*Teacher Created Resources, Inc.*

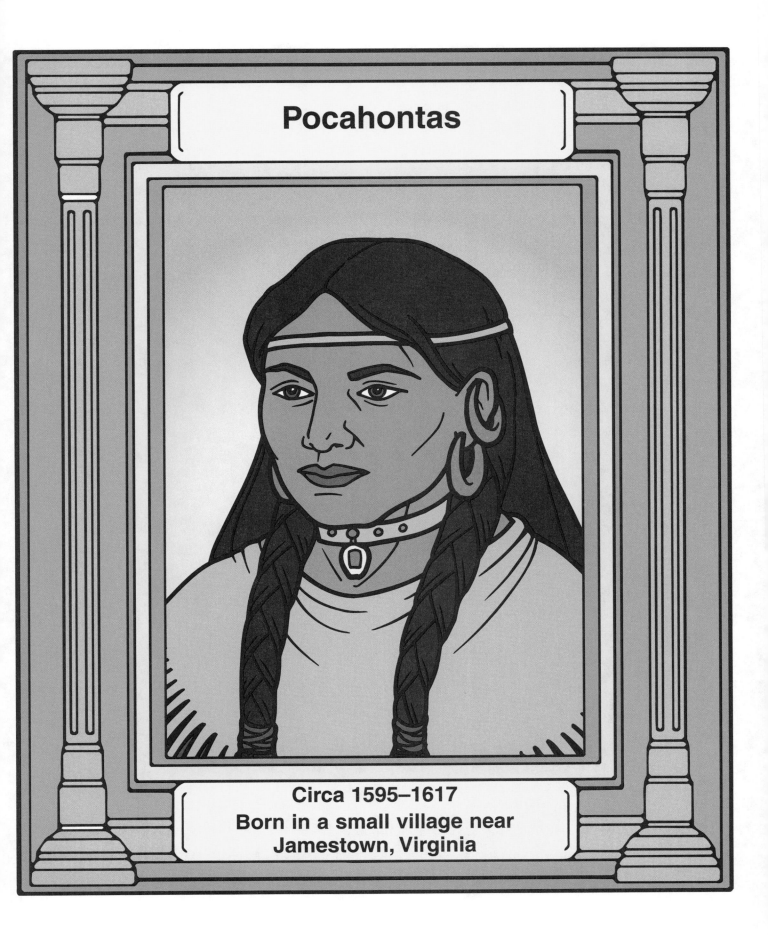

Pocahontas

Circa 1595–1617

**Born in a small village near
Jamestown, Virginia**

#3172 Social Studies Literacy Activities

Christopher Columbus

1451–1506
Born in Genoa, Italy

Martin Luther King, Jr.

1929–1968
Born in Atlanta, Georgia

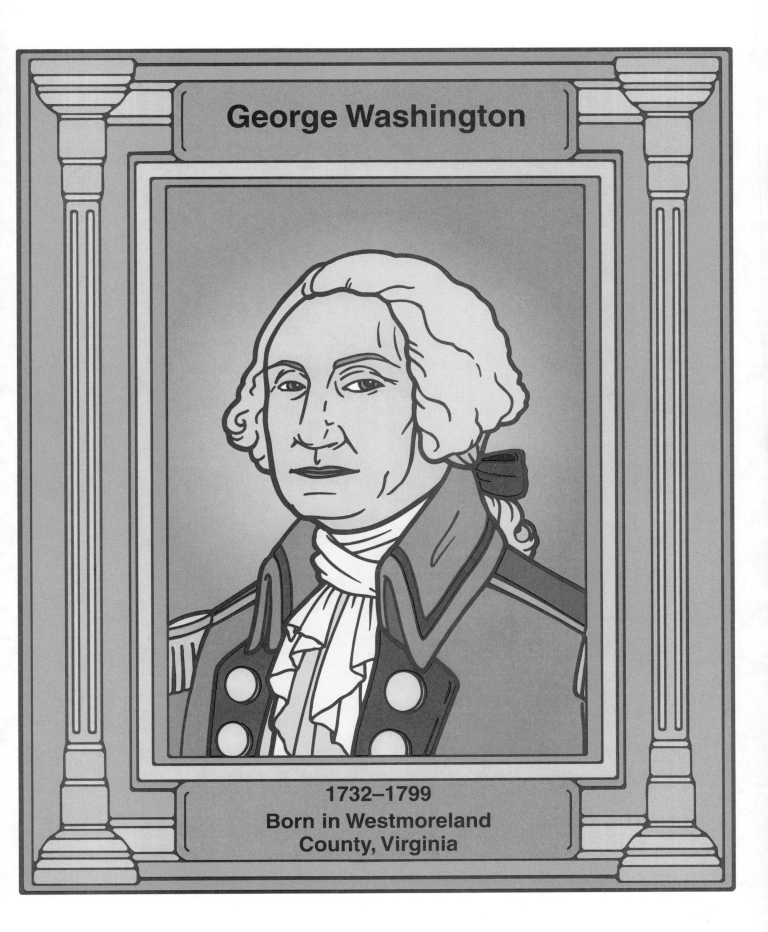

George Washington

1732–1799
Born in Westmoreland
County, Virginia

#3172 Social Studies Literacy Activities

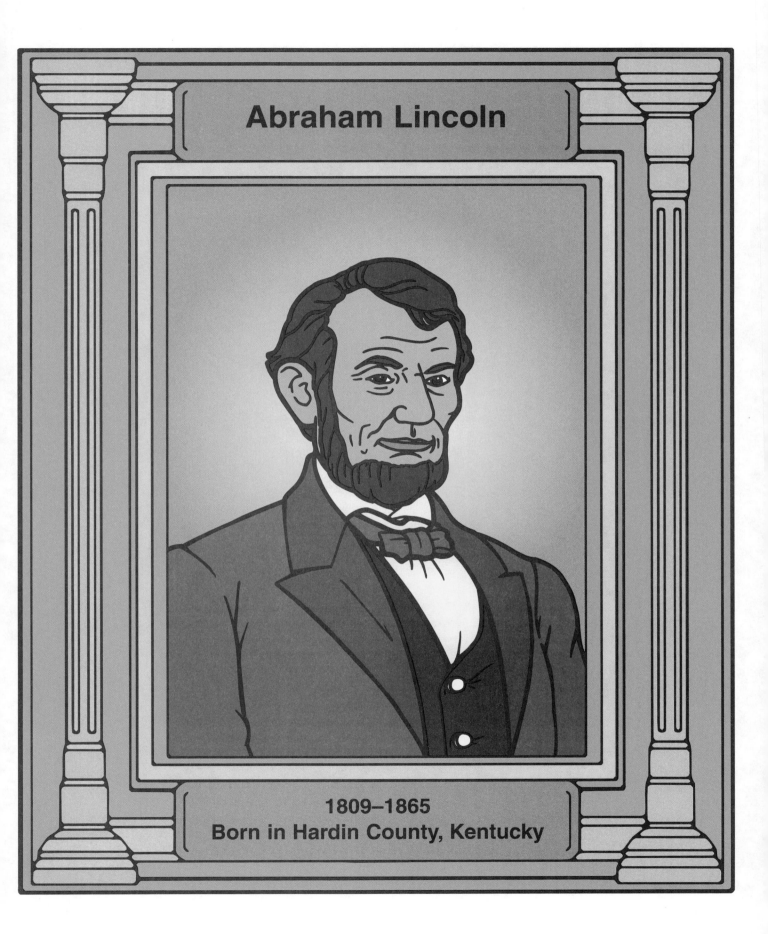

Abraham Lincoln

1809–1865
Born in Hardin County, Kentucky

#3172 Social Studies Literacy Activities

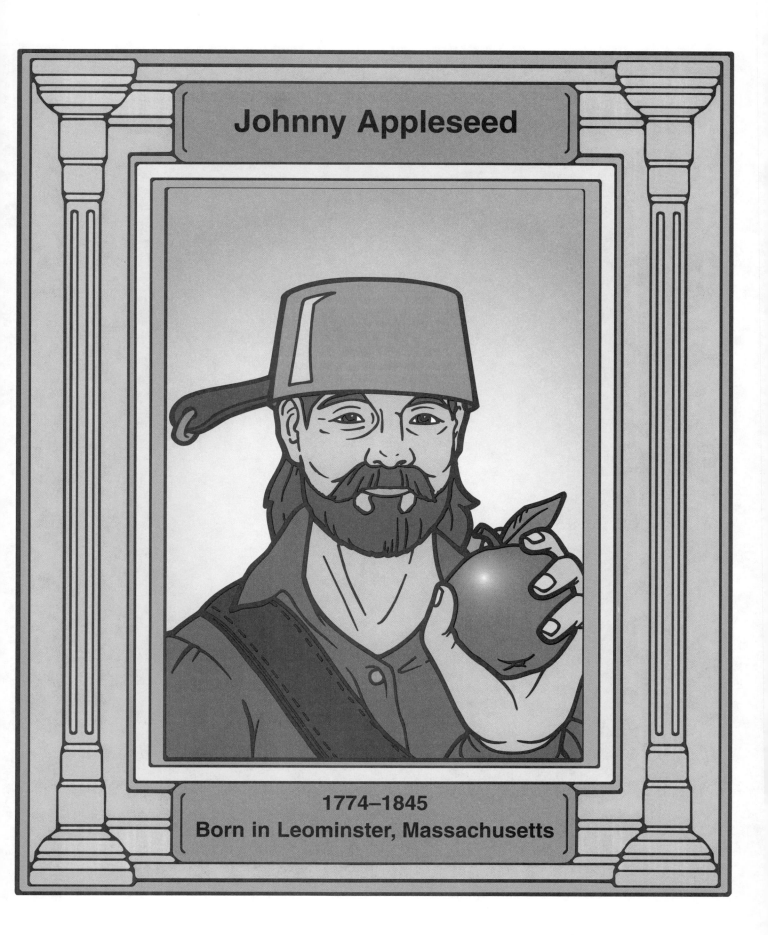

Johnny Appleseed

1774–1845
Born in Leominster, Massachusetts

#3172 Social Studies Literacy Activities

©*Teacher Created Resources, Inc.*

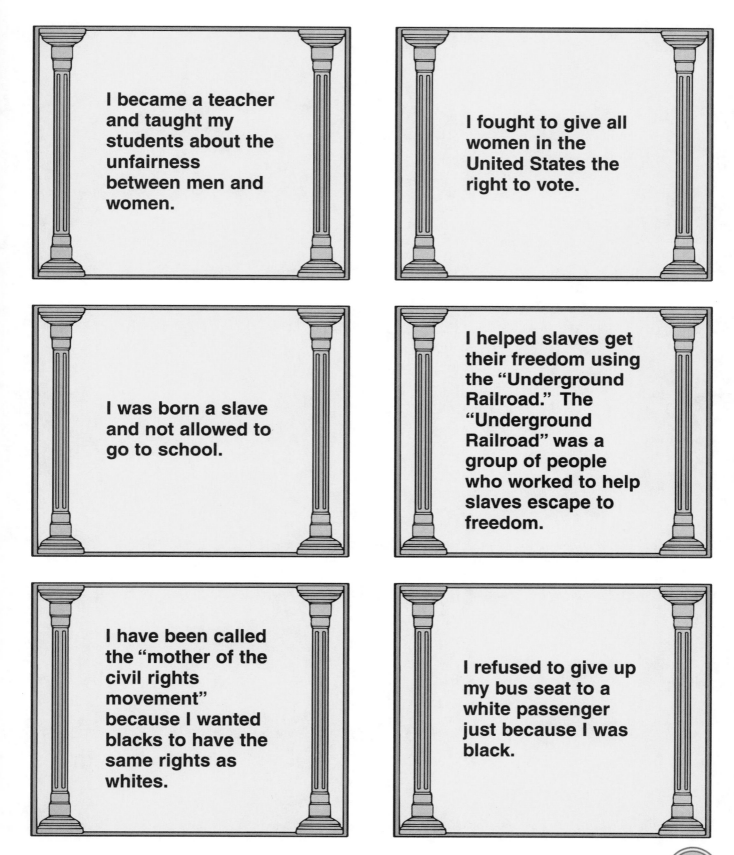

I became a teacher and taught my students about the unfairness between men and women.

I fought to give all women in the United States the right to vote.

I was born a slave and not allowed to go to school.

I helped slaves get their freedom using the "Underground Railroad." The "Underground Railroad" was a group of people who worked to help slaves escape to freedom.

I have been called the "mother of the civil rights movement" because I wanted blacks to have the same rights as whites.

I refused to give up my bus seat to a white passenger just because I was black.

#3172 Social Studies Literacy Activities

©*Teacher Created Resources, Inc.*

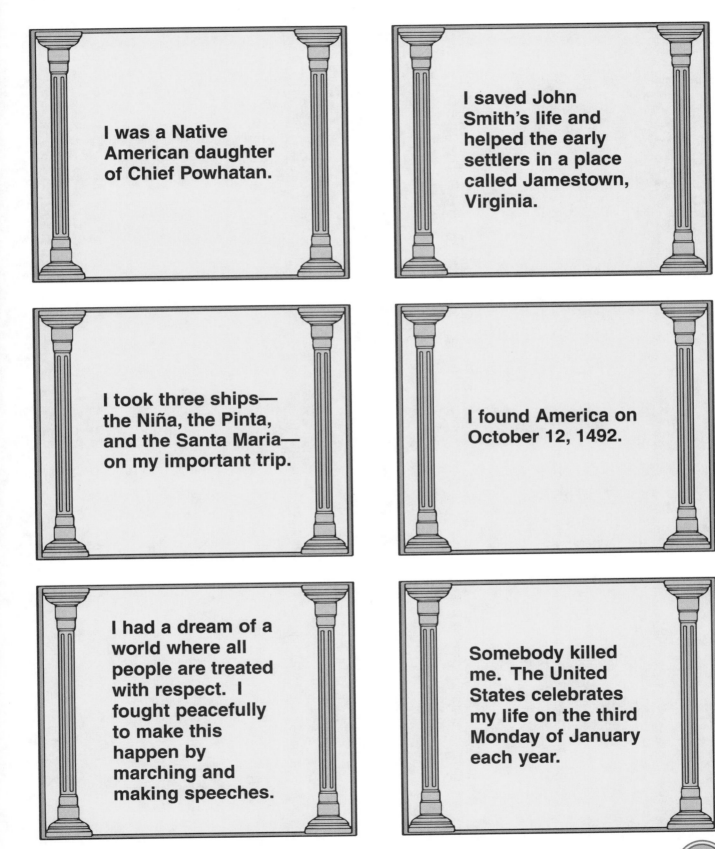

I was a Native American daughter of Chief Powhatan.

I saved John Smith's life and helped the early settlers in a place called Jamestown, Virginia.

I took three ships— the Niña, the Pinta, and the Santa Maria— on my important trip.

I found America on October 12, 1492.

I had a dream of a world where all people are treated with respect. I fought peacefully to make this happen by marching and making speeches.

Somebody killed me. The United States celebrates my life on the third Monday of January each year.

#3172 Social Studies Literacy Activities

#3172 Social Studies Literacy Activities

Fact Cards

I am seen on the one-dollar bill and the quarter.

I am known as the "Father of Our Country." I was the first president of the United States of America.

I was the sixteenth president of the United States. You can find my picture on the penny.

I signed an important paper, the Emancipation Proclamation, freeing all the slaves.

My name was really John Chapman. I lived a simple life. I liked to walk barefoot, wear sacks for clothes, and a tin pot for a hat.

I had a land full of apple orchards. I traveled to different states giving people bags full of apple seeds.

#3172 Social Studies Literacy Activities

Face to Facts Answer Key

 ## Susan B. Anthony

* I became a teacher and taught my students about the unfairness between men and women.
* I fought to give all women in the United States the right to vote.

 ## Harriet Tubman

* I was born a slave and not allowed to go to school.
* I helped slaves get their freedom using the "Underground Railroad." The "Underground Railroad" was a group of people who worked to help slaves escape to freedom.

 ## Rosa Parks

* I have been called the "mother of the civil rights movement" because I wanted blacks to have the same rights as whites.
* I refused to give up my bus seat to a white passenger just because I was black.

Pocahontas

* I am a Native American daughter of Chief Powhatan.
* I saved John Smith's life and helped the early settlers in a place called Jamestown, Virginia.

 ## Christopher Columbus

* I took three ships—the Niña, the Pinta, and the Santa Maria—on my important trip.
* I found America on October 12, 1492.

 ## Martin Luther King, Jr.

* I had a dream of a world where all people are treated with respect. I fought peacefully to make this happen by marching and making speeches.
* Somebody killed me. The United States celebrates my life on the third Monday of January each year.

 ## George Washington

* I am seen on the one-dollar bill and the quarter.
* I am known as the "Father of Our Country." I was the first president of the United States of America.

 ## Abraham Lincoln

* I was the sixteenth president of the United States. You can find my picture on the penny.
* I signed an important paper, the Emancipation Proclamation, freeing all the slaves.

 ## Johnny Appleseed

* My name was really John Chapman. I lived a simple life. I liked to walk barefoot, wear sacks for clothes, and a tin pot for a hat.
* I had a land full of apple orchards. I traveled to different states giving people bags full of apple seeds.

Ingenious Inventors Match

Skill

* understands major discoveries in science and technology and the major scientists and inventors responsible for them

Student Grouping

* individual
* partners
* small group
* large group (Make multiple copies of puzzle pieces.)
* center

Materials

* Puzzle Pieces (pages 73–79)

Directions

1. Explain to students that an invention is a new thing or a new way of doing something and that inventions can change our lives in big and small ways.

2. Brainstorm with students inventions and inventors.

3. Ask them what they might like to invent if they were inventors.

4. Tell them that they will learn about some very important inventors and their inventions.

5. Give students the puzzle pieces.

6. Have students study each of the puzzle pieces.

7. Tell them that they will match the inventor to the invention by joining the correct two puzzle pieces that fit together.

8. The activity is complete when all matches are found. You may want to encourage students to record the invention and inventor on a piece of paper.

Ideas

* Laminate puzzle pieces for durability.
* Have students become inventors. Ask them to develop something new. Have them write a description of their invention.

Puzzle Pieces

Alexander Graham Bell

telephone

Thomas Edison

light bulb

Orville and Wilbur Wright

airplane

#3172 Social Studies Literacy Activities

Puzzle Pieces

Levi Strauss

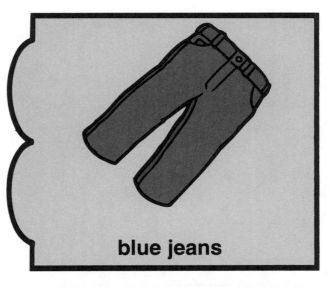

blue jeans

Elias Howe

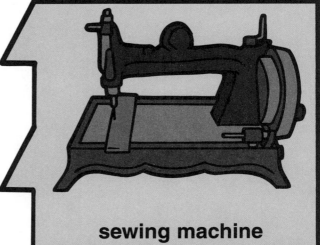

sewing machine

Benjamin Franklin

electricity

#3172 Social Studies Literacy Activities

©*Teacher Created Resources, Inc.*

Henry Ford

Model T

George Eastman

Kodak® Camera

Clarence Birdseye

frozen food

Puzzle Pieces

Percy Spencer

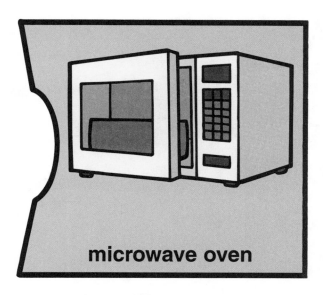

microwave oven

Louis Braille

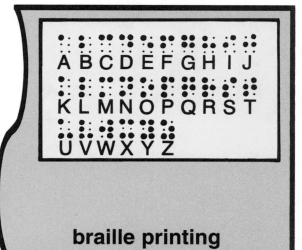

braille printing

Alfred Nobel

dynamite

#3172 Social Studies Literacy Activities

©*Teacher Created Resources, Inc.*

Now or Long Ago?

Skill

* compares items from now and long ago

Student Grouping

* individual
* partners
* small group (Copy more charts and item cards.)
* large group (Copy more charts and item cards.)

Materials

* Now or Long Ago? Sorting Chart (page 83)
* Now or Long Ago? Item Cards (page 85)
* chalkboard or whiteboard
* chalk or whiteboard marker

Directions

1. Discuss with students things that they noticed about themselves that have changed, such as height or clothing size.

2. Explain that today they will look at how some items have changed. They will decide which items are from a long time ago and which ones are from today.

3. Draw two columns on the board and label them Now and Long Ago.

4. Show students one item card as a sample. For instance, show the car from the past. Ask students, "Where do you think this car would go, under the title Long Ago or Now?" Ask students why it would be placed under Long Ago.

5. Have students mix up their item cards and place them in a pile facedown.

6. Students will pick an item card.

7. Then they will look at the card and decide whether it fits in the "Now" category or the "Long Ago" category on their charts.

8. Students will place each card under the appropriate heading.

9. Have students discuss why they placed them under the particular heading.

10. Continue until all item cards are categorized.

Ideas

* Have students bring in pictures of their families from the past. Have them discuss what is the same and what has changed.

* Have students interview older adults and record what things they used in the past that are different now, such as toys and clothing.

Sorting Chart

Long Ago	Now

#3172 Social Studies Literacy Activities

Item Cards

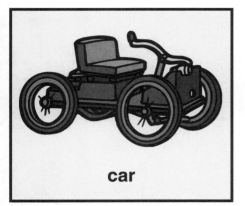

car

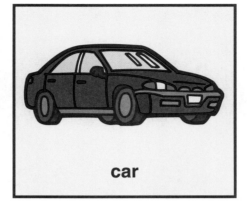

car

clothes

clothes

airplane

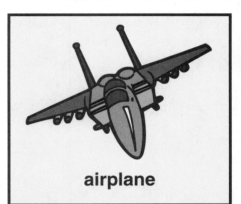

airplane

train

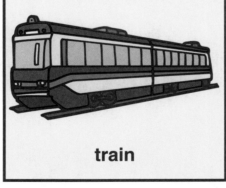

train

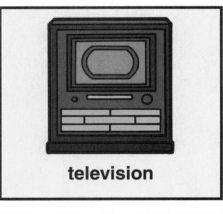

television

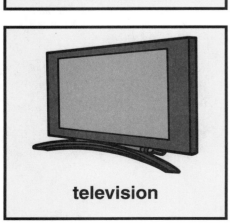

television

telephone

telephone

#3172 Social Studies Literacy Activities

©*Teacher Created Resources, Inc.*

Scenarios

Skill

* understands the importance for rules and discovers the reasons for them; understands that when rules are not followed, consequences will follow

 Student Grouping

* partners
* small group
* large group

Materials

* Situation Cards (page 89 and 91)

 Directions

1. Discuss with students the rules they have at home.

2. Ask them why they think rules are necessary.

3. Hand each group a Situation Card.

4. Explain that each set of partners (or small group) needs to act out what is happening in the card without telling the rule.

5. Give each group time to practice role-playing the situation. Allow some time for groups to develop props, if necessary.

6. Then have each group role-play the situation while the other groups observe.

7. After the group is finished performing, discuss with the students what the rule is and why the rule is necessary. Also, discuss whether the rule is being followed. If it is not being followed, discuss with the students what the consequence might be.

8. Repeat the same procedure with all the other groups.

9. For closure, discuss with students the rules in the classroom and why they are important.

Ideas

* Laminate Situation Cards for durability.

* As a variation, give each group a Situation Card and write about what is happening in the picture and whether or not the rule is being followed. Have them write why the rule would be important and what might happen if the rule was not followed.

* Have each student write the rules he or she would have in the classroom if he or she was the teacher and why.

* Have students create posters for each rule in the classroom and post them as reminders.

* Have students discuss with parents the rules that adults have to follow—such as stopping at stop signs or driving the speed limit—and the reasons for them. Have adults also discuss the consequences of adults not following those rules.

Situation Cards

Rule: Clean things you use.

Rule: Walk inside the crosswalk.

Rule: Raise your hand when you want to speak.

Rule: Share things with others.

Rule: Show respect toward other people's things.

Rule: Walk inside the classroom.

Situation Cards

Rule: Do not talk to any strangers.

Rule: When you are upset, use your words.

Rule: Put trash inside the waste basket.

Rule: Hang up your jackets.

Rule: Wash your hands after using the restroom.

Rule: Listen to your teacher.

#3172 Social Studies Literacy Activities

Let's Take a Vote

Skill

* understands how the political system of the U.S. operates and provides opportunity for participation

Student Grouping

* partners
* small group
* center

Materials

* Voting Choice Cards (pages 95 and 97)
* Voting Ballots (page 99 and 101)
* decorated shoebox labeled "Ballot Box" with slit on top through which to place voting ballots
* writing utensils or dry erase markers (See Ideas section below.)

Directions

1. Explain to students that in the United States, people choose the leader of the country by voting. One leader that is chosen by voting is the President. Tell them that people might also vote for or against a law or plan.

2. Tell students that today they will get to make a choice and vote.

3. Tell them to pretend that their class received some extra money. They must make a choice for spending the extra money.

4. Show the two Voting Choice Cards and read the text on them. Explain the two choices: (A) Spend the money on books and build a bigger class library; or (B) Spend the money on more classroom writing supplies such as colored pencils, crayons, markers, etc. Then students can have more supplies to use when writing.

5. Prompt students to think about important questions such as "Which do we need more—books or writing supplies?" or "Which choice will help everybody?"

6. Pass out the ballots. Tell students that a ballot records a person's vote and that the choice with the most votes will win.

7. Explain to students that now it is time to record their votes. Have each student record his or her vote on the ballot. Remind them that each student must make only one choice.

8. Students then walk to the ballot box and place their ballots inside the box.

9. Show the results of the votes in a tally graph. Talk about which plan received more votes and possible reasons why. Also, have students share which choice they made and why.

Ideas

* Laminate the ballots. Have the ballots available with dry erase markers so ballots can be wiped clean and used over again.

* Make some voting booths using decorated cardboard pieces, and have students record their votes in them.

* Talk about the President's jobs (Example: helps to keep our country safe). Ask them what character qualities would make a good choice for President.

Choice A

- Buy more books for our class.

- This will help make the classroom library bigger.

Choice B

- Buy more class writing supplies.
- This will help students have more supplies to use when writing.

#3172 Social Studies Literacy Activities

©*Teacher Created Resources, Inc.*

Voting Ballots

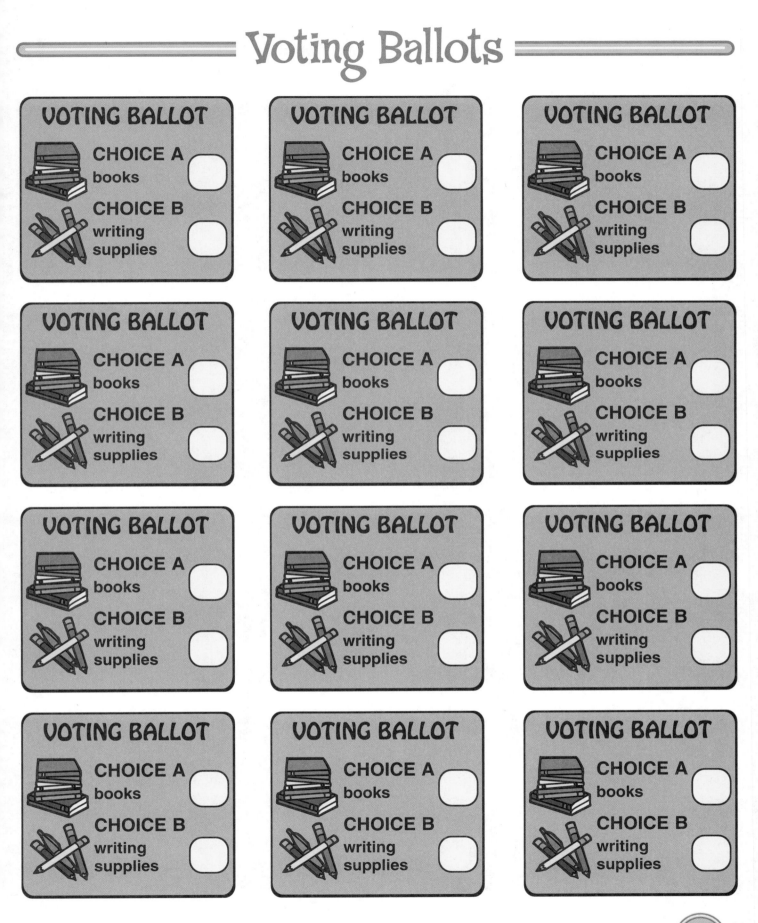

Voting Ballots

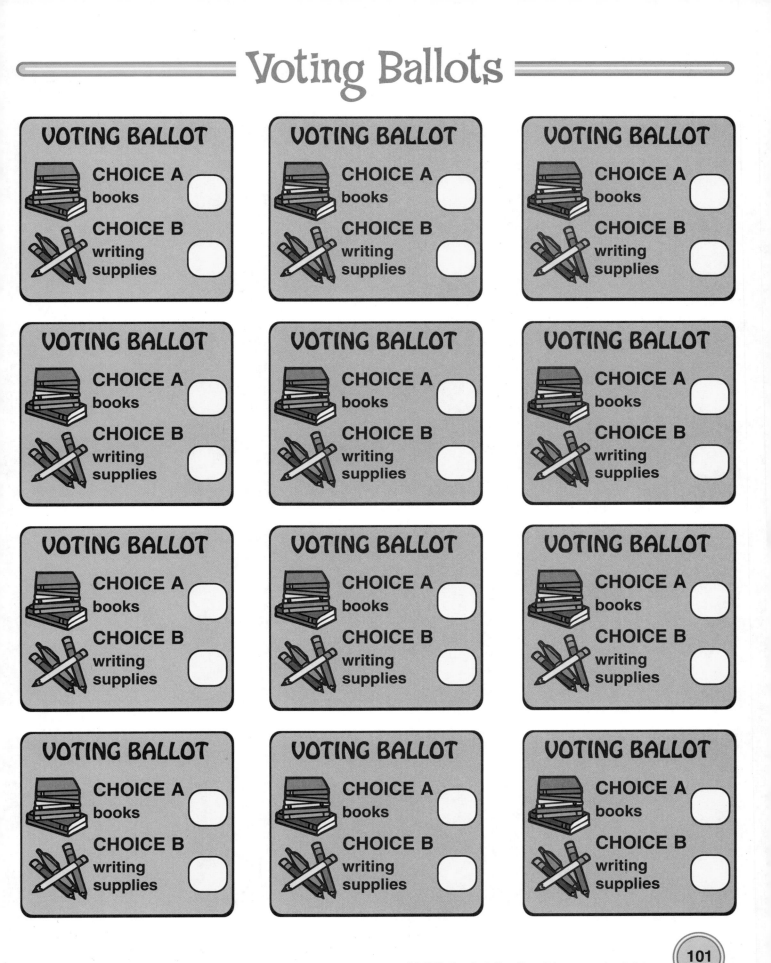

Transportation Classification

Skill

* understands the many types of transportation used to move people and products

Student Grouping

* independent
* partners
* center
* small group
* large group

Materials

* chalk or whiteboard marker
* chalkboard or whiteboard
* Classification Chart (page 105)
* scissors (*optional*)
* glue (*optional*)
* Transportation Cards (page 107)

Directions

1. Brainstorm with students the different ways people travel.

2. Ask students what different ways they have traveled.

3. Tell students that you can put these different ways into groups—land, air, and water.

4. Write the three categories—Land, Air, Water—on the board.

5. Give one example—such as a car—and discuss what category it would fall under.

6. Give students a copy of the Classification Chart and the Transportation Cards.

7. Have students place each card under the appropriate category. (*Option:* If students have their own personal Classification Chart and Transportation Cards, students can cut and glue the cards under the appropriate category. However, remind them to have their answers checked before gluing.)

Ideas

* Laminate chart and cards, especially when using in a center.

* Discuss the differences between the ways people travel now and how they traveled long ago.

* Have students interview their family members and find out ways they traveled when they were young.

* Have students take a chart home. Have students classify and write on the chart all the different ways of transportation they saw during one week. Have students share their charts.

* Have students look through magazines and cut out pictures of different types of transportation. Students then glue pictures to paper and make transportation collages.

Classification Chart

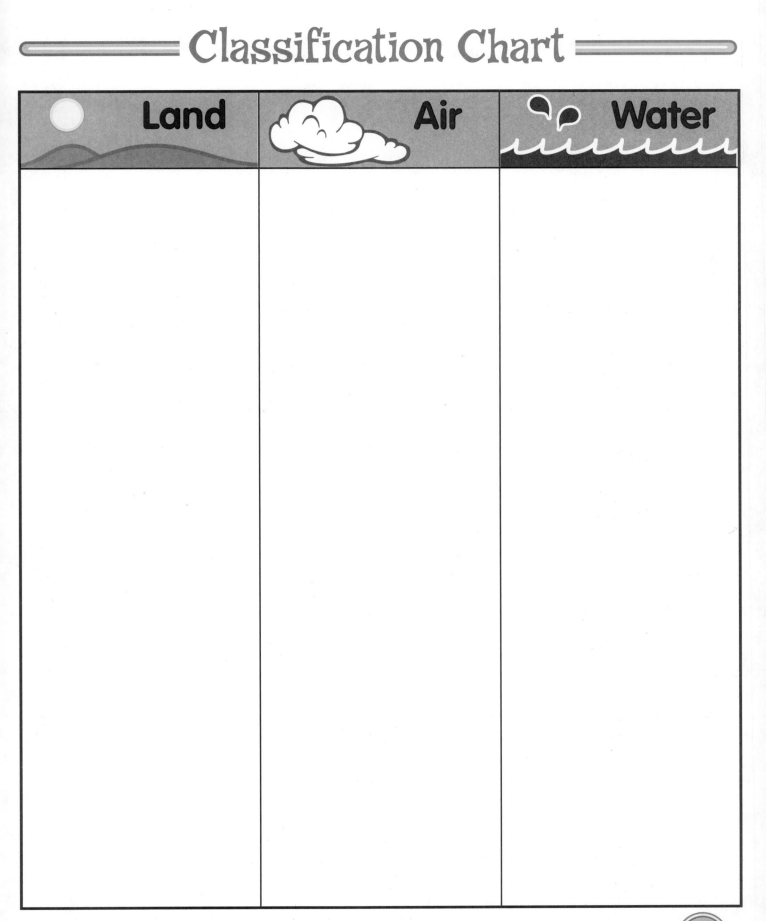 Land	Air	Water

Transportation Cards

truck	spaceship	bus
bike	airplane	hang glider
helicopter	sailboat	ferry
fishing boat	train	hot air balloon
cruise ship	canoe	carriage

#3172 Social Studies Literacy Activities

©*Teacher Created Resources, Inc.*

Corny or Bananas?

Skill

* locating the origin of food items found in the local stores by tracing their routes from place of origin

Student Grouping

* individual

* partners

* small group

* large group (*Note:* Make multiple copies of materials.)

Materials

* Food Flow Chart (page 111)

* puzzle pieces for corn (page 113) or bananas (page 115)

Directions

1. Brainstorm with students why food is important and how we need food to live. Then ask the students from where they think the food they eat comes.

2. Explain that much of the food we eat comes from farms. Tell them that farms are places where people grow plants or raise animals, and each farm can be different.

3. Tell students that they will get a chance to put together a food puzzle that shows how food gets from the farm to the store.

4. Show the Food Flow Chart. Show students where the flow chart begins and how it flows to the end.

5. Choose the puzzle pieces for the corn or for the bananas.

6. Give students puzzle pieces.

7. Have students try to place the pieces in the correct order—start to end—on the Food Flow Chart.

Ideas

* Laminate Food Flow Chart and puzzle pieces, especially when using in a center.

* Have students bring to the classroom items that they eat and find out from where they come. Try using a map to plot the areas where the products were made.

* Bring in many food products and have students classify which items come from plants and which items come from animals.

* Discuss with students all the modes of transportation that can be used to get food to the store. (See Transportation Classification on page 103.)

Food Flow Chart

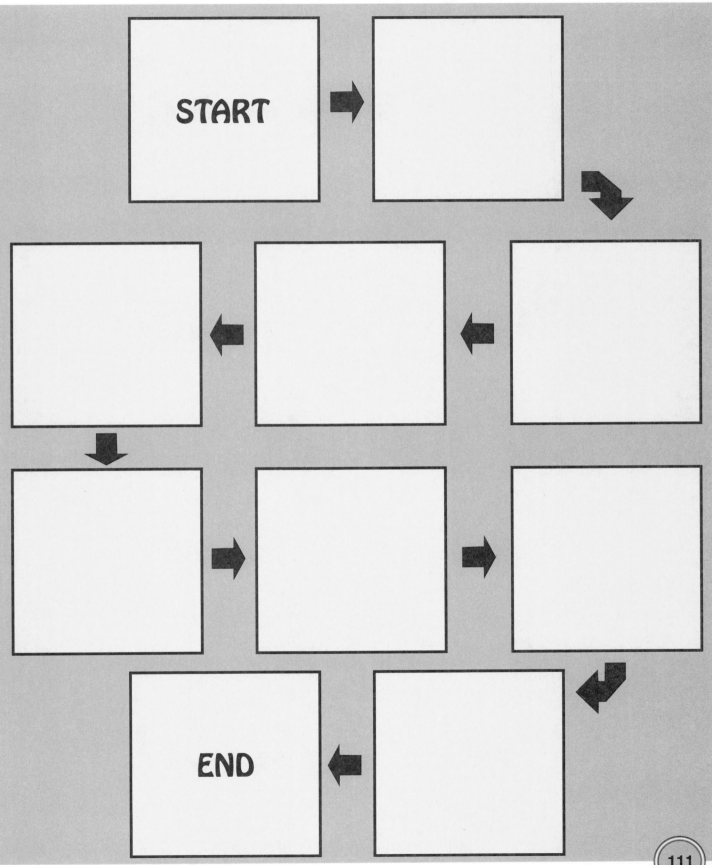

#3172 Social Studies Literacy Activities

©*Teacher Created Resources, Inc.*

Corn

A farmer plants seeds of corn.

The seeds start to sprout.

The seeds become plants.

The plants grow ears of corn.

The corn is picked off the plant.

The corn goes to a factory.

Happy Farms
CORN

The corn is put in a package.

The corn travels to the store.

FROZEN FOODS

The corn is put on a shelf to be sold.

The corn is bought and eaten.

#3172 Social Studies Literacy Activities

Bananas

Most banana plants are grown on banana plantations outside of the United States.

The workers pick the bananas when they are green.

The bananas are then taken to a packing plant.

The workers cut bunches of bananas off the large stem.

The workers carefully put the bananas into the boxes.

The boxes then travel by a train to a nearby seaport.

The bananas are then put onto a ship going to the United States.

The bananas are put on a truck going to a warehouse where they will ripen.

The truck takes the bananas to the store.

The bananas are bought and then eaten.

#3172 Social Studies Literacy Activities

©*Teacher Created Resources, Inc.*

Can't Do Without You

Skill
* understands the effects of specialization and interdependence of people

Student Grouping
* individual
* partners
* large group
* center
* small group

Materials
* Community Workers cards (pages 119 through 133)
* paper (optional)
* pencils (optional)
* Who Am I? Cards (page 135)

Directions
1. Brainstorm with students what people they depend on in their city or town (Examples: doctor, police, etc.).
2. Tell them to imagine a town or city without these people. Ask them what it would be like.
3. Explain to them that each person has a special job, and we depend on him or her to do his or her job.
4. Show each picture card to the students.
5. Have students write or discuss what important job the person in the card is doing and in what ways we depend on him or her. Mention that these people are also dependent on one another. (Optional: Read each of the Who Am I? Cards and have students guess the occupation.)

Ideas
* Ask students what occupation they would like to have and describe the reason why.
* Have each student write a story about one person on one of the cards. For example, he or she could write about all the jobs of a fire fighter.
* Have students role-play a community of workers.
* Have students create additional cards for other occupations. Have them explain how the person in the card contributes to the community. Make a Community Workers book which includes all of the student-created cards.
* Use the Community Workers cards to supplement other social studies lessons.

Community Workers

teacher

#3172 Social Studies Literacy Activities

Community Workers

grocer

fire fighter

#3172 Social Studies Literacy Activities

Community Workers

doctor

mail carrier

Community Workers

sanitation worker

#3172 Social Studies Literacy Activities

©Teacher Created Resources, Inc.

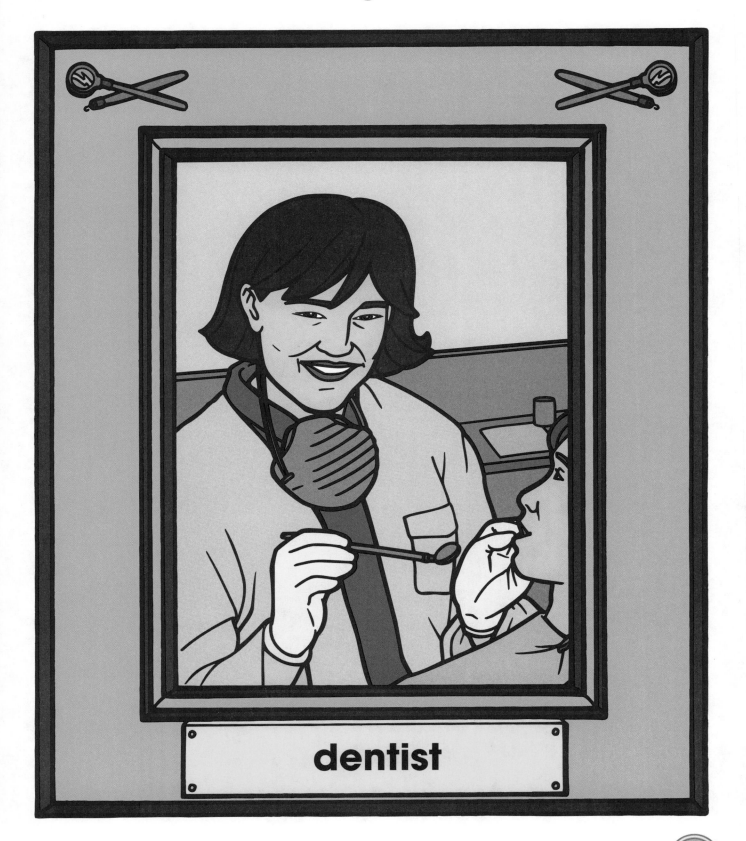

dentist

#3172 Social Studies Literacy Activities

police officer

Who Am I? Cards

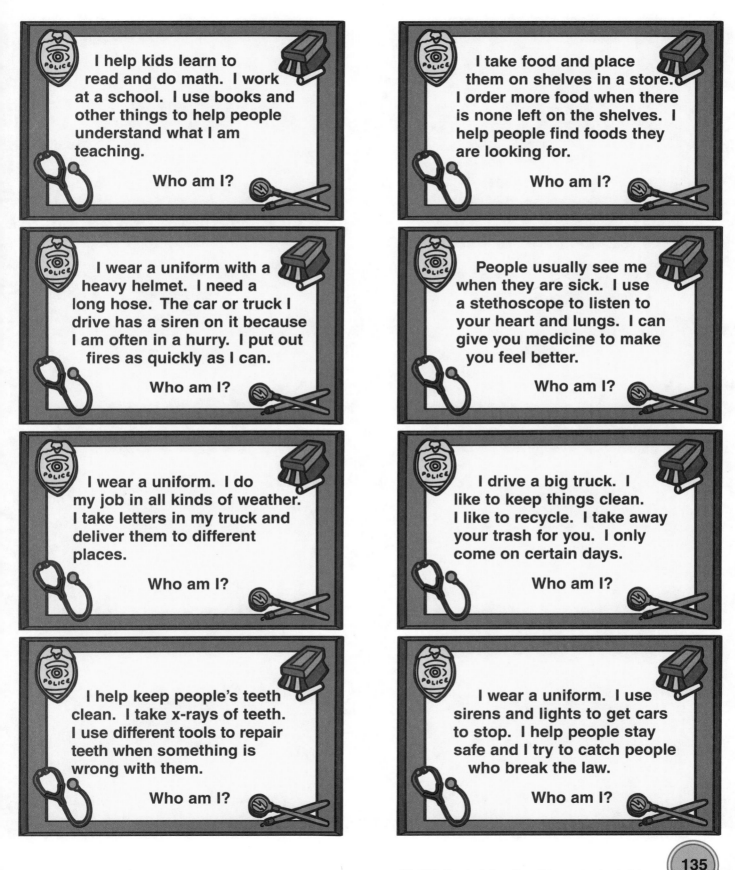

I help kids learn to read and do math. I work at a school. I use books and other things to help people understand what I am teaching.

Who am I?

I take food and place them on shelves in a store. I order more food when there is none left on the shelves. I help people find foods they are looking for.

Who am I?

I wear a uniform with a heavy helmet. I need a long hose. The car or truck I drive has a siren on it because I am often in a hurry. I put out fires as quickly as I can.

Who am I?

People usually see me when they are sick. I use a stethoscope to listen to your heart and lungs. I can give you medicine to make you feel better.

Who am I?

I wear a uniform. I do my job in all kinds of weather. I take letters in my truck and deliver them to different places.

Who am I?

I drive a big truck. I like to keep things clean. I like to recycle. I take away your trash for you. I only come on certain days.

Who am I?

I help keep people's teeth clean. I take x-rays of teeth. I use different tools to repair teeth when something is wrong with them.

Who am I?

I wear a uniform. I use sirens and lights to get cars to stop. I help people stay safe and I try to catch people who break the law.

Who am I?

Magnificent Maps

Skill

* knows how to use a map key to interpret symbols and cardinal directions to locate places

Student Grouping

* independent
* partners
* center
* small group
* whole group

Materials

* Classroom Map (page 139), School Map (page 141), Neighborhood Map (page 143), or Community Map (page 145)
* pencils (*optional*)
* paper (*optional*)

Directions

1. Choose one of the following maps that is appropriate for your students' level:

   * classroom
   * school
   * neighborhood
   * community

2. Explain that maps show how places look from above.

3. Give each student a copy of the map.

4. Discuss the elements on the map such as symbols, map key, or a compass rose.

5. Have students answer questions that are located below the map on a piece of paper or answer the questions together as a group. (Note: Answers are located on the back of each map.)

Ideas

* Laminate each map and place it in a center.
* For beginning-level students, have them map something simple, such as things on their desks.
* Have students make their own classroom, neighborhood, or community map using symbols, compass rose, and/or a map key.

Classroom Map

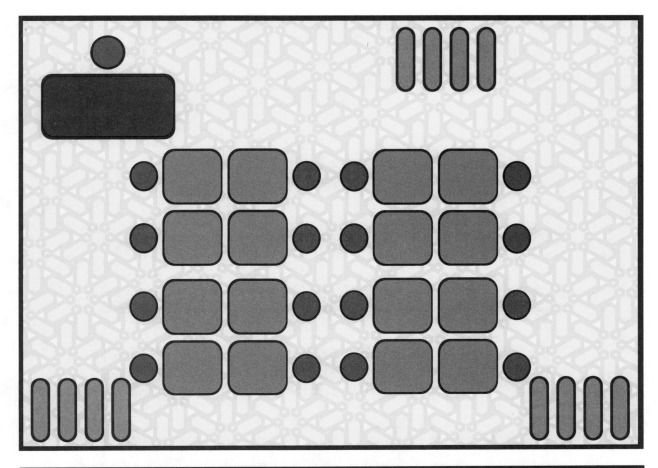

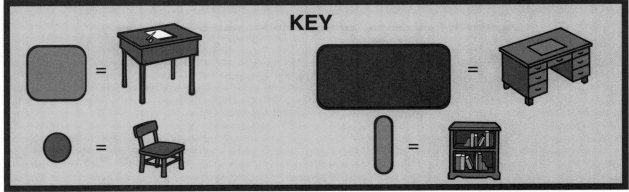

KEY

Questions

1. What is ?

2. What is ?

3. How many are there?

Answers

1. student desk

2. bookshelf

3. 17 chairs

School Map

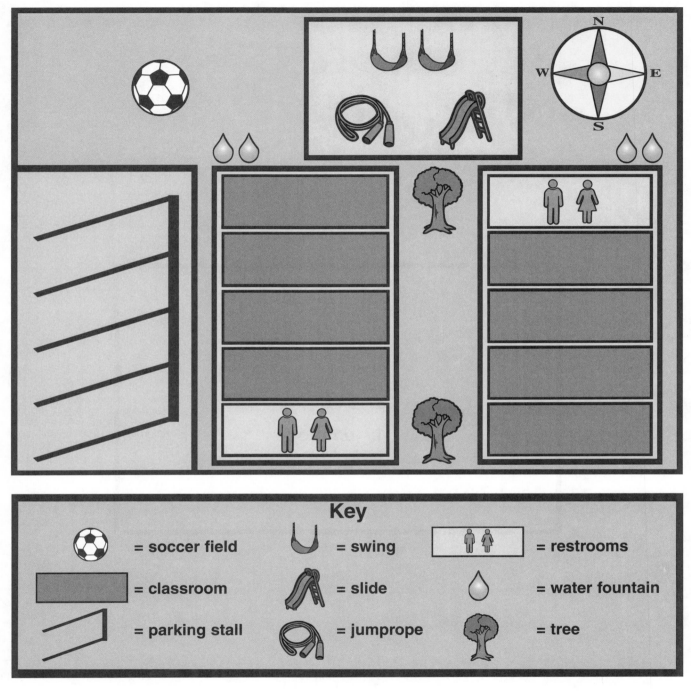

Key

 = soccer field

= swing

= restrooms

= classroom

= slide

= water fountain

= parking stall

= jumprope

= tree

Questions

1. How many parking stalls?

2. How many classrooms?

3. How many swings?

4. What is [jumprope] ?

5. What is [restrooms] ?

6. What is north of the parking stall?

#3172 Social Studies Literacy Activities

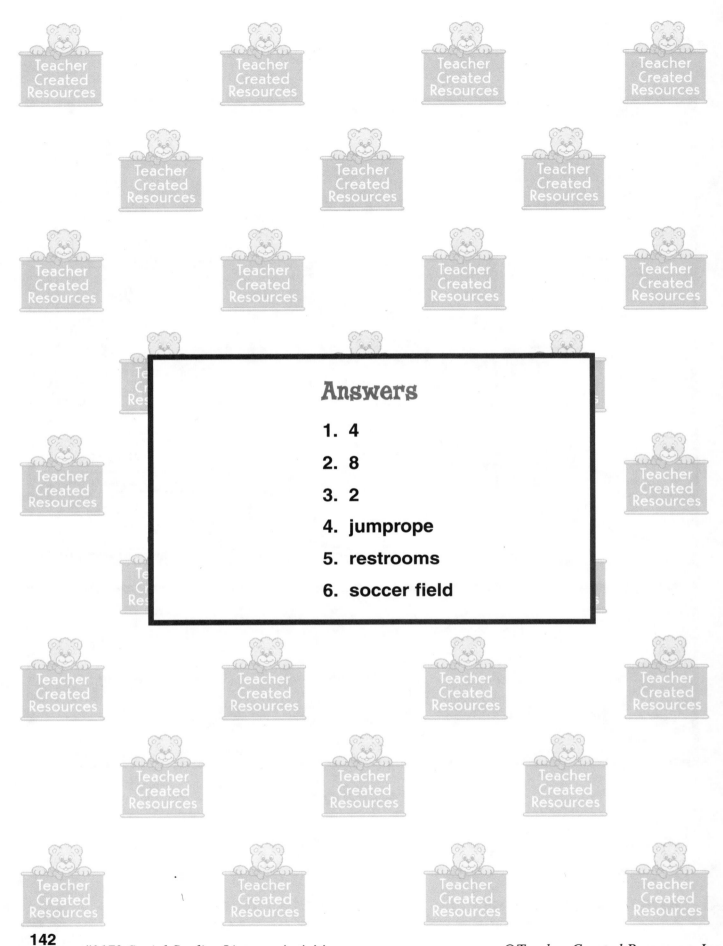

Answers

1. 4
2. 8
3. 2
4. jumprope
5. restrooms
6. soccer field

Neighborhood Map

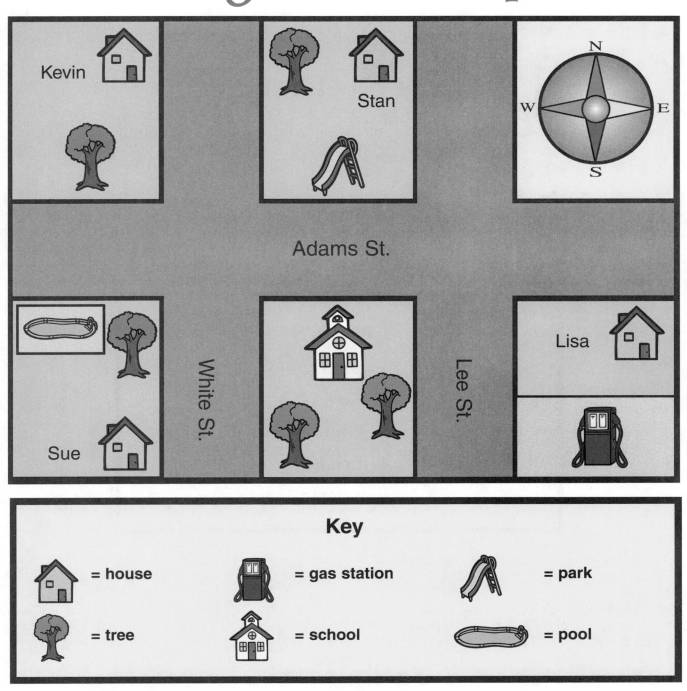

Key

= house   = gas station   = park

= tree   = school   = pool

Questions

1. Who lives east of Kevin?

2. Who lives north of Sue?

3. On which street does Sue live?

4. On which street is the gas station?

5. On which street is the park?

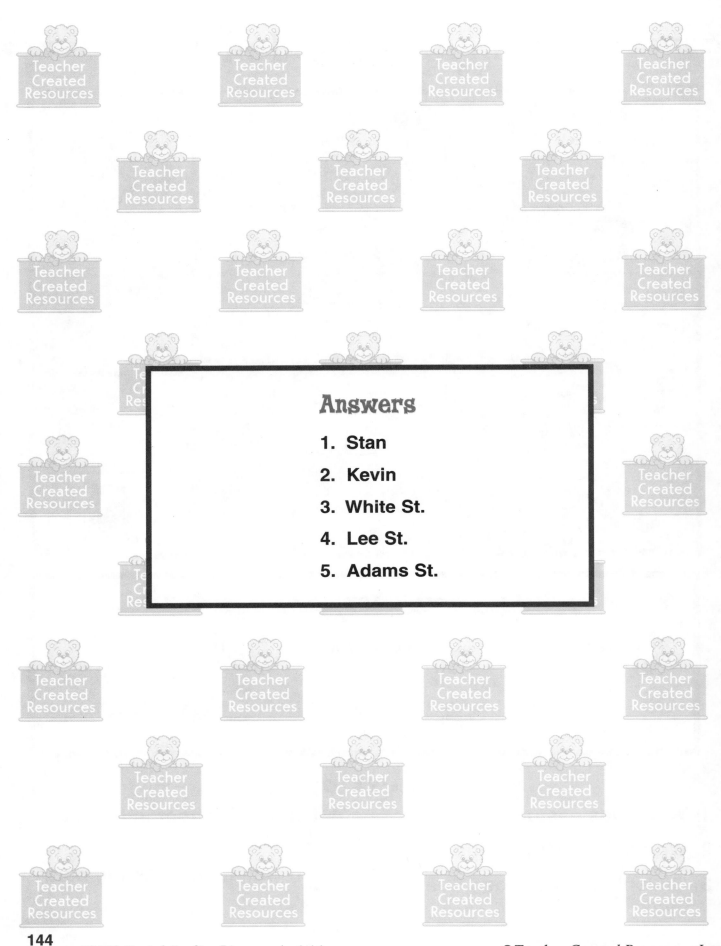

Answers

1. **Stan**
2. **Kevin**
3. **White St.**
4. **Lee St.**
5. **Adams St.**

Community Map

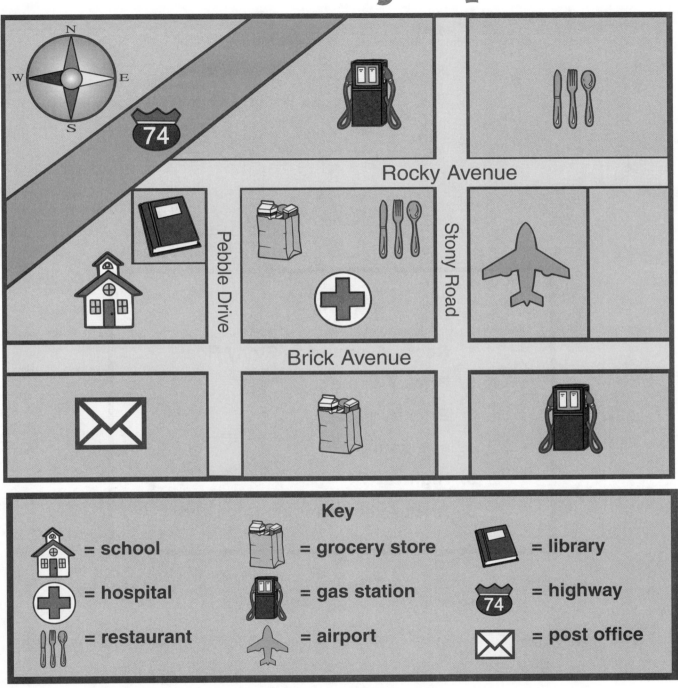

Key

= school

= grocery store

= library

= hospital

= gas station

= highway

= restaurant

= airport

= post office

Questions

1. On what streets are the the restaurants located?

2. On what street is the school located?

3. On what street is the hospital located?

4. What place is north of the airport?

5. What highway runs through this community?

6. What are the nearest cross streets to the post office?

©*Teacher Created Resources, Inc.*

#3172 Social Studies Literacy Activities

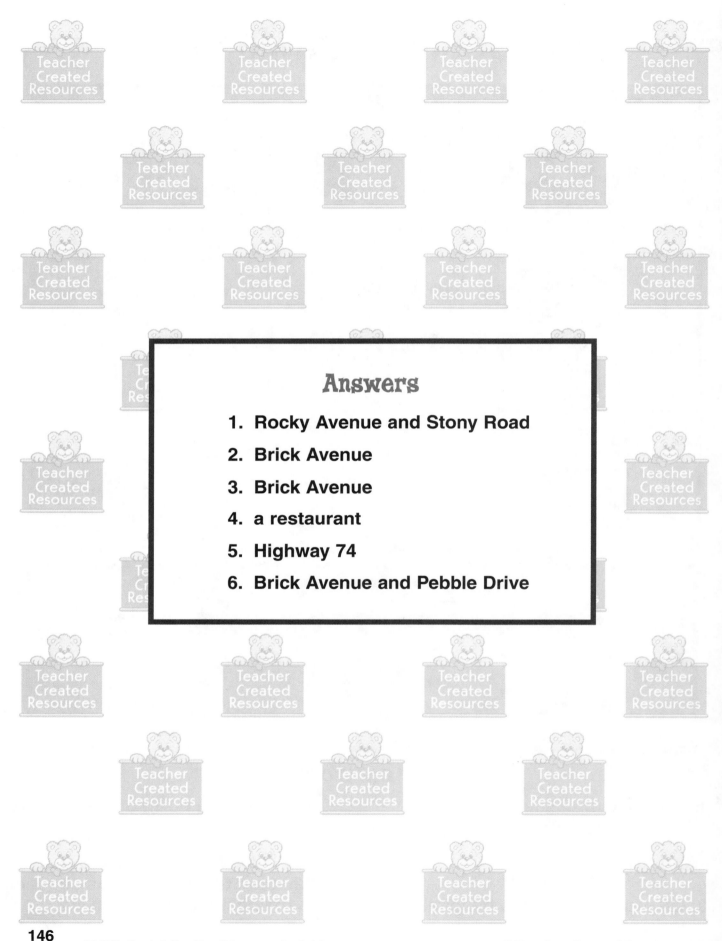

Answers

1. **Rocky Avenue and Stony Road**
2. **Brick Avenue**
3. **Brick Avenue**
4. **a restaurant**
5. **Highway 74**
6. **Brick Avenue and Pebble Drive**

What a Wonderful World!

Skill

* names and locates continents, countries in North America, oceans, and the United States on a map

Student Grouping

* independent
* partners
* small group
* whole group
* center

Materials

* Choose one of the following maps on which to focus: North America Map (page 149), World Map (pages 154 and 155), or United States Map (pages 160 and 161). Then make a copy of the particular map for each student. (*Note:* Make color copies, if possible. Laminate them for future use. You may also use maps available in the classroom.)
* copies of worksheets that accompany the particular chosen map—North America Questions (page 151), World Questions (page 157), or United States Questions (page 163)
* Answer Key for all questions (page 148)
* pencils

Directions

1. Explain to students that a map shows where things are located.
2. Give students one of the following maps (depending on which map will be the focus and which level is most appropriate for your students): North America, world, or United States.
3. Study the map together and encourage discussion about all the different parts and what they symbolize. At this time, you may want to introduce vocabulary such as *state*, *country*, *continent*, *ocean*, etc.
4. Give each student a copy of the matching worksheet.
5. Have students independently, in partners, or in small groups answer the questions on the worksheet.
6. Have students check their answers with the answer key.

Ideas

* Laminate all maps for future use.
* Have students create more questions about the map and record them on the back of their worksheets.
* Cut up the question squares on the worksheets and laminate them to use for a center along with the matching map. Also, attach the matching answer key for students to check their answers independently.
* After students are finished with the activity, have them choose a partner to ask questions about the map. For example, if using the United States map, a student can ask another student to name a state beginning with the letter **T**.
* Have students describe in what state, country, and continent they are living, using the map.
* Use a map to locate where certain foods and products used by students and their families are produced.

Answer Key

Answers for North America Questions (page 151)

1. North America

2. compass rose

3. ocean or sea

4. Pacific Ocean, Atlantic Ocean

5. Canada

6. Mexico

Answers for World Questions (page 157)

1. world

2. Pacific, Atlantic, Arctic, or Indian Ocean

3. North America, South America, Africa, Europe, Asia, Australia, or Antarctica

4. North America

5. Arctic Ocean

6. Equator

Answers for United States Questions (page 163)

1. United States

2. Answers will vary.

3. Minnesota, Michigan, Montana, Missouri, Mississippi, Maine, Maryland, or Massachusetts

4. Pacific Ocean

5. Atlantic Ocean

6. Canada

#3172 Social Studies Literacy Activities

North America Map

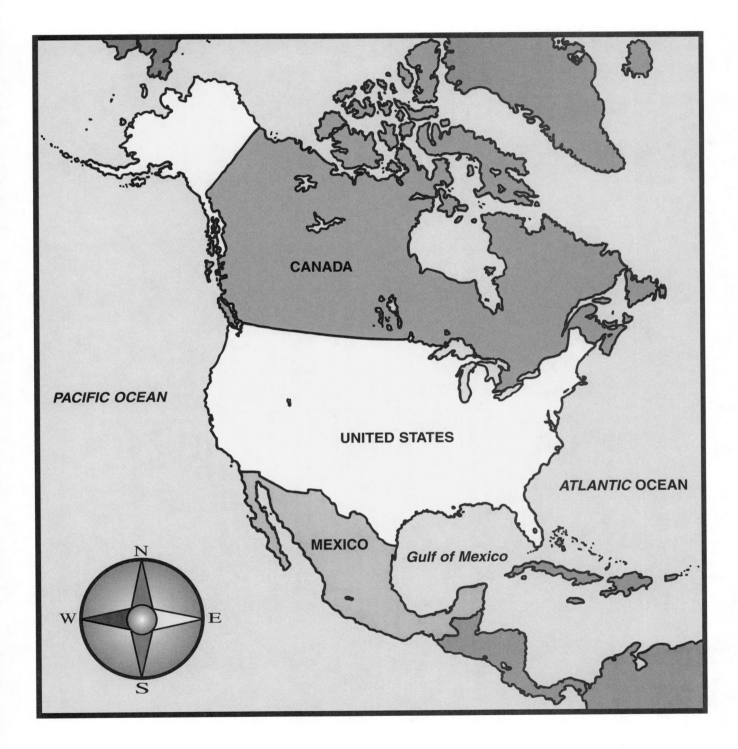

North America Questions

Name_____

1. This is a map of what?

_____

2. What is 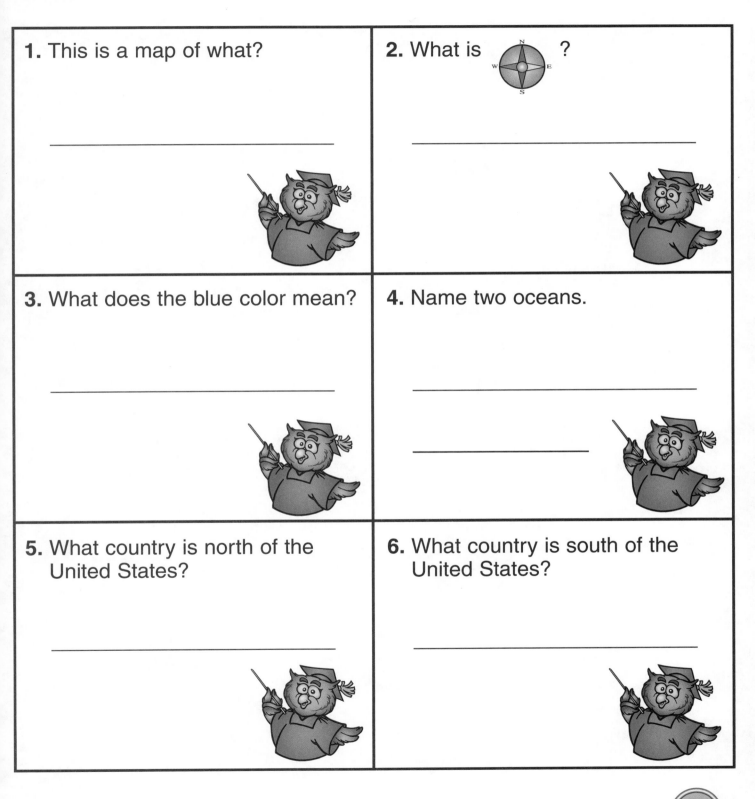 ?

_____

3. What does the blue color mean?

_____

4. Name two oceans.

_____

_____

5. What country is north of the United States?

_____

6. What country is south of the United States?

_____

#3172 Social Studies Literacy Activities

#3172 Social Studies Literacy Activities

World Map

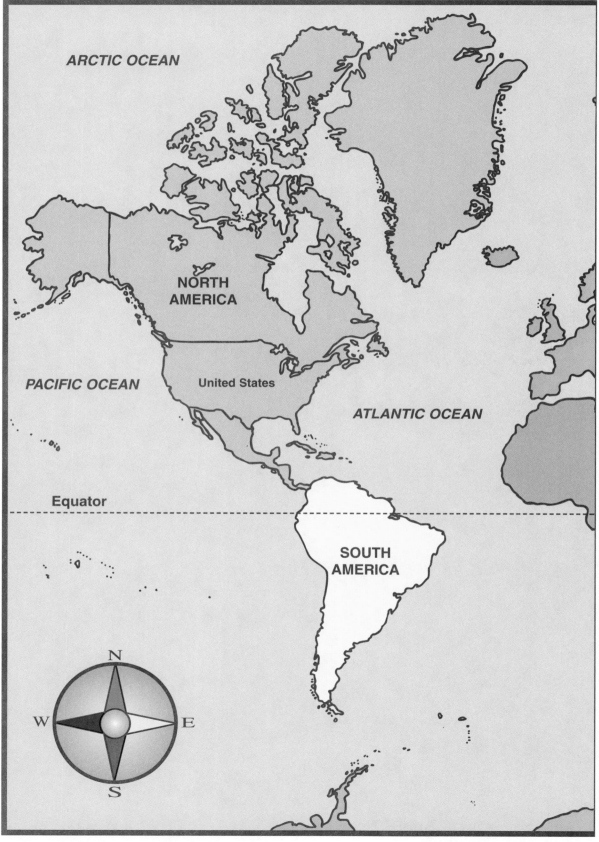

ARCTIC OCEAN

NORTH
AMERICA

PACIFIC OCEAN

United States

ATLANTIC OCEAN

Equator

SOUTH
AMERICA

N

W   E

S

World Map

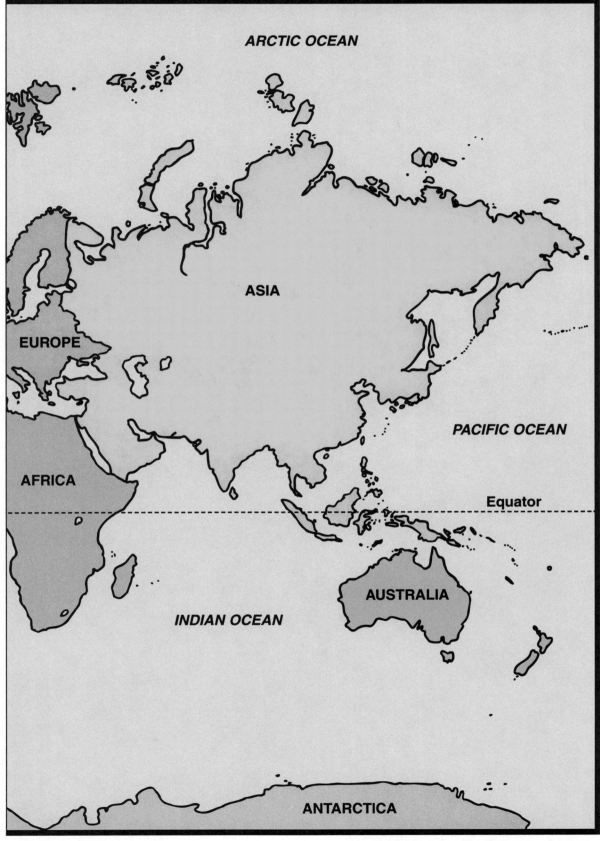

ARCTIC OCEAN

ASIA

EUROPE

AFRICA

PACIFIC OCEAN

Equator

AUSTRALIA

INDIAN OCEAN

ANTARCTICA

#3172 Social Studies Literacy Activities

World Questions

Name_____

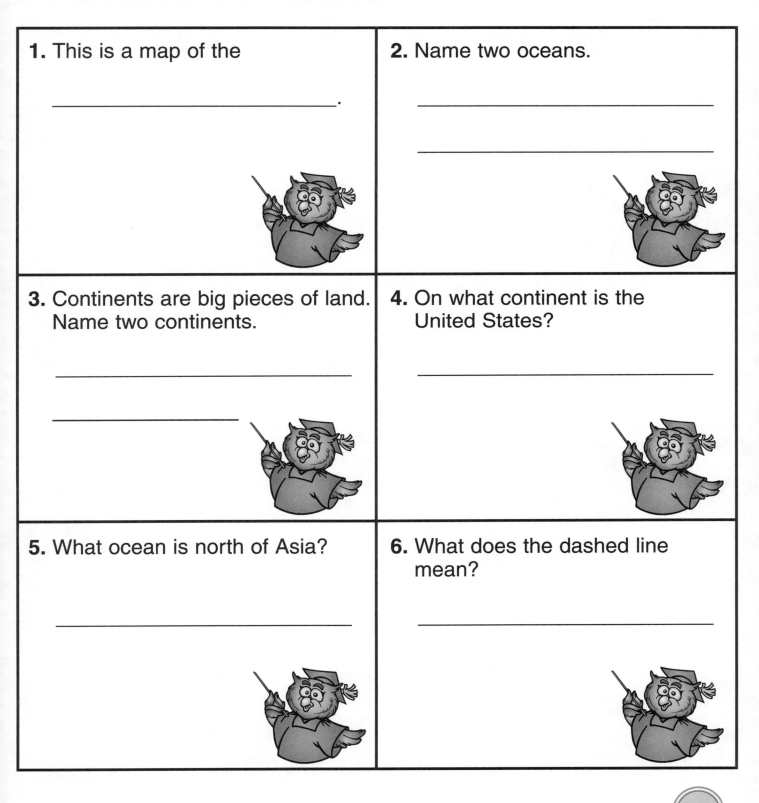

1. This is a map of the

_____.

2. Name two oceans.

_____

_____

3. Continents are big pieces of land. Name two continents.

_____

_____

4. On what continent is the United States?

_____

5. What ocean is north of Asia?

_____

6. What does the dashed line mean?

_____

United States Map

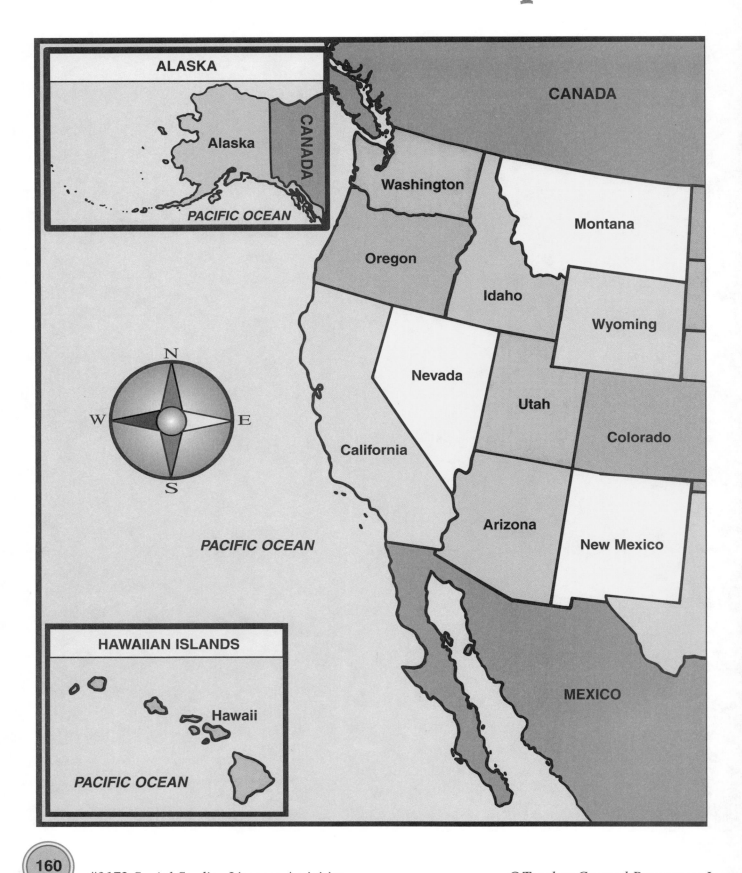

ALASKA

Alaska

CANADA

PACIFIC OCEAN

CANADA

Washington

Oregon

Montana

Idaho

Wyoming

Nevada

Utah

Colorado

California

Arizona

New Mexico

N

W E

S

PACIFIC OCEAN

MEXICO

HAWAIIAN ISLANDS

Hawaii

PACIFIC OCEAN

United States Map

CANADA

Vermont

Massachusetts

Lake Superior

Maine

New Hampshire

North Dakota

Minnesota

South Dakota

Wisconsin

Lake Michigan

Michigan

Lake Huron

Lake Ontario

New York

Rhode Island

Iowa

Lake Erie

Pennsylvannia

Nebraska

Illinois

Indiana

Ohio

West Virginia

Connecticut

Kansas

Missouri

Kentucky

Virginia

New Jersey

Oklahoma

Arkansas

Tennessee

North Carolina

Delaware

Maryland

South Carolina

Texas

Mississippi

Alabama

Georgia

Louisiana

Florida

ATLANTIC OCEAN

Gulf of Mexico

#3172 Social Studies Literacy Activities

United States Questions

Name_____

1. This is a map of the

   _____.

2. There are 50 states in the United States. Name two states.

   _____

   _____

3. Name two states that start with the letter M.

   _____

   _____

4. What ocean is to the west of the United States?

   _____

5. What ocean is to the east of the United States?

   _____

6. What country is to the north of the United States?

   _____

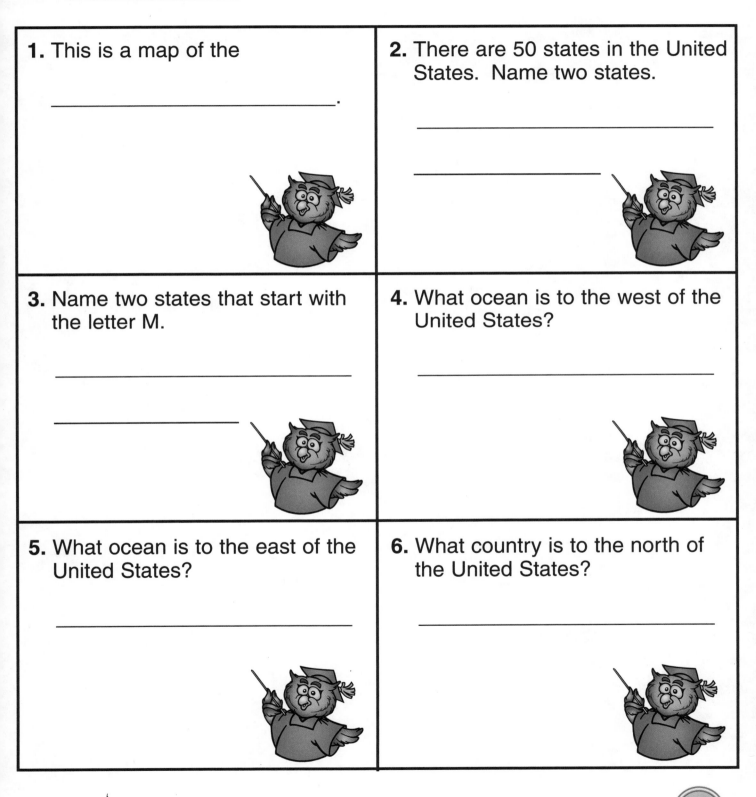

#3172 Social Studies Literacy Activities

#3172 Social Studies Literacy Activities

Valuable Vocabulary

Skill

* recognizes basic geographical terms, such as *desert, hill*, etc.

Student Grouping

* independent

* partners

* small group

* center

Materials

* Geography Vocabulary cards precut (pages 167–173)

* Answer Key (page 175)

Directions

1. Lay all picture cards on a flat surface face up so all pictures are visible to all players.

2. Mix up all the definition cards and place them in a pile face down.

3. Have Player 1 pick one card and read the definition (or have a teacher or fluent reader read the definition).

4. Player 1 tries to find the matching picture card.

5. The match is checked against the Answer Key. If the match is correct, Player 1 keeps the match. If it is incorrect, the picture card is returned with the other picture cards and the definition card is returned to the bottom of the pile.

6. Player 2 then proceeds with his or her turn and repeats the same process.

7. The winner is the person with the most matches.

Ideas

* Laminate cards for durability, especially when using in a center.

* Have students make their own geography vocabulary cards. They can add more geography terms, such as *gulf* or *canyon*.

* Have students make a dictionary of geographical terms.

* Have students make 3-D models of various land forms.

Geography Vocabulary

salt water that covers a lot of the earth

a flow of water that goes to an ocean or lake

salt or fresh water that has land all around it

a large piece of earth or rock rising out of the land

trees and plants that cover a large piece of land

a piece of land that has water all around it

#3172 Social Studies Literacy Activities

Geography Vocabulary

ocean or sea

river

lake

mountain

forest

island

Geography Vocabulary

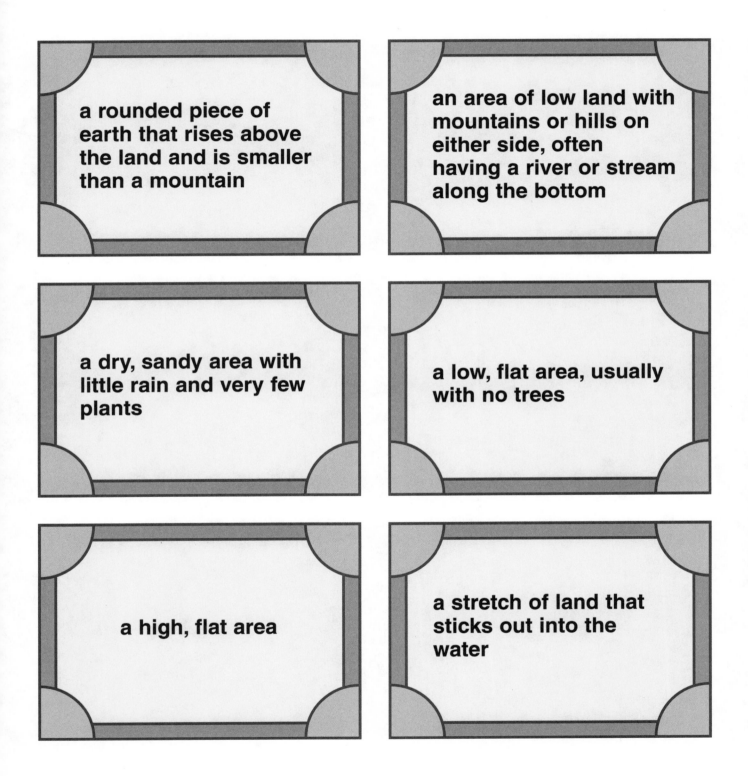

a rounded piece of earth that rises above the land and is smaller than a mountain

an area of low land with mountains or hills on either side, often having a river or stream along the bottom

a dry, sandy area with little rain and very few plants

a low, flat area, usually with no trees

a high, flat area

a stretch of land that sticks out into the water

#3172 Social Studies Literacy Activities

Geography Vocabulary

hill

valley

desert

plain

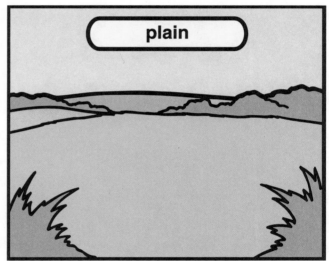

plateau

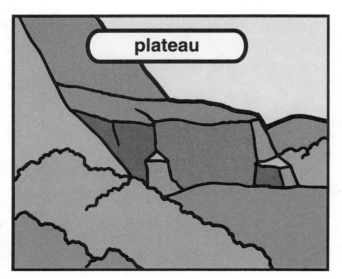

peninsula

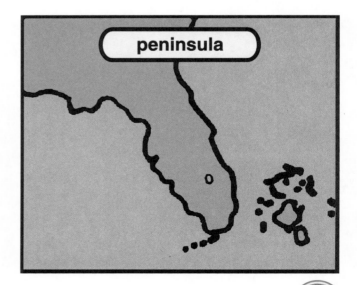

#3172 Social Studies Literacy Activities

Answer Key

ocean or sea = salt water that covers a lot of the earth

river  = a flow of water that goes to an ocean or lake

lake = salt or fresh water that has land all around it

mountain = a large piece of earth or rock rising out of the land

forest = trees and plants that cover a large piece of land

island = a piece of land that has water all around it

hill = a rounded piece of earth that rises above the land and is smaller than a mountain

valley = an area of low land with mountains or hills on either side, often having a river or stream along the bottom

desert = a dry, sandy area with little rain and very few plants

plain = a low, flat area, usually with no trees

plateau = a high, flat area

peninsula = a stretch of land that sticks out into the water